I0487887

Achieving Process Profitability

Achieving Process Profitability

Building the IT Profit Center

Gregory J. Deckler

iUniverse, Inc.

New York Lincoln Shanghai

Achieving Process Profitability
Building the IT Profit Center

iUniverse, Inc.

For information address:
iUniverse, Inc.
2021 Pine Lake Road, Suite 100
Lincoln, NE 68512
www.iuniverse.com

ISBN: 0-595-28970-3

Contents

Preface

I wrote this book because I believe that the incredible success of information technology (IT) within business has resulted in the demise of the core mission of IT. It seems that the real purpose of computers and technology within business has been lost. Where once Personal Computers (PCs) and PC networks were hailed as time savers and productivity boosters, the reality and expense of managing hundreds or thousands of PC's all networked together has caused companies to view PC's and PC networks more along the lines of a cost of doing business rather than a way to do business more effectively, efficiently and profitably. Businesses today are more concerned with controlling IT costs rather than the true mission of IT. And while companies should be concerned about controlling IT costs, they should not make decisions based solely upon cost and at the expense of IT's single, universal and undeniable mission.

The reason this situation has come to pass stems directly from the phenomenal success of PC's and PC networks. The success and resulting ubiquity of PC's and PC networks within business has resulted in many businesses forgetting life without the PC and the PC network. Companies now seem to view PC's, PC networks and IT in general simply as cost centers. Computers are simply there and must be supported but the reason why they are there is no longer widely understood within the daily operations of a business.

This fundamental misunderstanding of IT has now led to tremendous amounts of people in the world doing IT badly. And by badly, I do not mean simply providing poor service and systems, but fundamentally missing the boat when it comes to understanding the role and value of IT to a business. This core, fundamental misunderstanding is the root cause of many of the ills within the IT industry including the product and vendor-centric focus of IT, poor service and a fundamental lack of understanding with regards to business process.

A good illustration of this point is the stereotypical view people have of IT personnel. A perfect illustration of this is Jimmy Fallon's portrayal of the condescending *"Nick Burns, Your Company's Computer Guy,"* on *Saturday Night Live*. I am not saying that all stereotypes are true to life, but I have been in the IT business long enough and am honest enough to admit that the attitudes and actions

"Nick Burns" portrays towards his end users is closer to reality than fiction for many in IT.

The focus on cost control within IT has led to IT becoming more of a monolithic, tyrannical bureaucracy whose sole purpose is to dictate standards in order to control IT support costs. This perception has not been helped by the central role that standards play within IT. In IT, there are standards for everything under the sun and so it is not hard to see why many in IT have latched onto standards as their central mission in life. But, in doing so, many have forgotten that there is more to IT than just creating and enforcing standards.

I wrote this book to serve as a reminder of the role of IT within business and to show businesses what they should be looking for and demanding from their IT systems and departments. Now, I am not saying that I have all of the answers to all of the ills within IT. I have been an IT consultant for nearly all of the 15 years that I have been an IT professional and have consulted for literally dozens of global companies, including Owens Corning, Tricon Global Restaurants (KFC, Pizza Hut, Taco Bell), Procter & Gamble, Marathon Ashland Petroleum, Hilton Hotels, etc. In this time, I have seen IT done extremely well and I have seen IT done extremely poorly. And there are common threads among the good IT departments as well as common threads among the bad IT departments. By being an independent observer to scores of different IT departments in my career, I have been able to objectively watch and see what certain departments do well and what they do poorly. This book is a compilation of some of the conclusions I have reached after more than a decade of such observation and work.

If you are in IT, then I implore you to wipe your mind clean of your preconceived notions and read this book with an open mind. If you are not in IT, do not be put off by the IT theme that runs throughout this book. I believe that everyone that runs, manages or is involved in the daily affairs of a business needs to understand and master the concepts, ideas and observations contained within this book. This book was written with that audience in mind, not just CIO's.

Introduction

The acronym IT stands for Information Technology. But what does this really mean? There may very well be no single, universal definition of IT. Heck, as ironic as it may seem, people cannot even agree on an acronym, Information Services (IS) and IT are used interchangeably. Regardless, for the purposes of this text, we assume that when people discuss "IT", what they are talking about are computers and other digital systems within a business. Telephones and other odds and ends of technology get thrown in as well as things like mainframes, mini's, etc.

The most visible components of IT that most people deal with in their daily lives are personal computers (PC's). Personal computers and the networking technologies that grew up around them revolutionized modern businesses and their impact cannot be understated or underestimated. But why? Why have personal computers and networking had such a tremendous impact on modern business? This core, fundamental question is at the heart of this book because many of the observations and much of the analysis within this book are predicated upon the answer to this question.

In order to fully understand the role of IT within a business, why IT has had such a tremendous impact on businesses and ultimately, where IT has gone wrong, we must look back at the reason why computers and technology were invented and became such a crucial component of modern businesses. Now, I am not going to bore you with a bunch of useless nostalgia about the history of computers. In all honesty, who really cares about the *ENIAC* or the *Apple II* or the *Osborne I*? Yeah, yeah, yeah a bunch of old hardware that is useless and embarrassing in today's world. Instead, I am going to select a particular item/event out of the entirety of computer history and narrowly analyze it in order to prove a point.

To set the stage, we will dial the clock back to the late Seventies. Although computers had already been around for decades, they were mainly used for research and for games, not business. All this changed around 1980 or so. All of a sudden, the personal computer burst onto the business scene and nothing has been the same since. Now, there were many factors involved in exactly why this occurred, but I would argue that the single most important development that caused the PC revolution was none other than the spreadsheet. The original spreadsheet, *VisiCalc* came onto the scene in 1979 and the next was *SuperCalc* in 1980. By 1985 *Lotus 1-2-3* had gained dominance and today the leading spreadsheet is *Microsoft Excel*.

Now, this is not a big revelation, the link between the development of the spreadsheet and the proliferation of the computer within business is old hat to most computer professionals. The spreadsheet was the original "killer app". It provided a reason for accountants and business people to buy a personal computer. In fact, the *Osborne I* probably owed a large part of its success to the fact that each *Osborne I* shipped with a free copy of *Supercalc*.

Now back to why. Why did spreadsheets cause such a ruckus? The answer is quite simple, because spreadsheets gave accountants and business people a better, more efficient, and more effective way to do their jobs. Complex calculations could be performed simply by entering numbers and formulas into the cells of a spreadsheet. If a number changed, instead of potentially spending hours re-calculating numbers, the spreadsheet could re-calculate the numbers in seconds. Spreadsheets made accountants and other business people so productive that it justified the considerable expense of a personal computer in the time, effort and money saved. Quite simply, it made businesses more profitable having a computer and spreadsheet than not having a computer and spreadsheet.

So, what conclusions can be drawn from this observation? First, the reason computers succeeded in business in the first place was due to simple economics. A business was more profitable having a computer and spreadsheet than not having a computer and spreadsheet. The second item that I would point out is the importance of software. Without software, a computer is a glorified piece of silicon (sand) and just as worthless. Sure, one must have a computer to run software, but the computer hardware itself is of secondary importance. People buy a computer in order to do something with it, not just simply to have it. Third, spreadsheets were a simple and elegant tool that lent themselves to easy customization by end users. And end users were enormously inventive at adapting spreadsheets to automate business processes that would otherwise take many hours of manual labor.

There is a tremendous amount that can be learned from these three simple conclusions and I will refer back to them throughout this book. These three fundamental conclusions form the basis of why computers initially succeeded within business and still serve as the basis for making computers (IT) successful within a business. In fact, these three conclusions are so fundamental and important that I will go so far as to formalize them…

The Three Canons of IT:

1. IT must make economic sense

2. IT is about software automating manual tasks

3. IT must be useable

1

The Mission of IT

There is a single, universal and undeniable mission for IT. This mission has remained the same ever since PC's burst onto the business scene twenty plus years ago. However, before delving into this mission, let us first look at those things that are commonly propped-up as the mission for IT and debunk the myths surrounding them. These myths have at their heart a fundamental, fatal flaw that will prevent companies and individuals that embrace these myths as their mission from accomplishing their goals and succeeding in business.

IT Myth #1

IT's mission is to ensure that a business's computer and technology systems work

While this might seem like a rational and reasonable mission, it is nothing of the kind. The mistake here is in mistaking the job of IT with its mission. One of IT's jobs is to ensure that a business's computer and technology systems work. However, this is far from the mission of IT. The mistake is a common one and it is easy to fall into the trap of merging one's mission with one's job. However, it is particularly important that one realize the difference between the job of IT and the mission of IT.

Failure to understand the difference between one's job and one's mission leads to many of the ills associated with bad IT. A particular ill effect of viewing IT's mission as one of ensuring the operation of a business's computer and technology systems is that this view leads to IT becoming a monolithic standards body that is solely concerned with dictating and enforcing standardized systems throughout a business.

Think of this in terms of traveling. Let's say that you need to make a business trip from Columbus, OH to Chicago, IL. And let's further speculate that you decide to make that trip in your car. Saying that IT's mission is to ensure that a

1

business's computer and technology systems work is like saying that your mission, in this example, is to drive your car. Driving your car is not the mission. Your mission is to get from Columbus, OH to Chicago, IL. Your job is to drive the car.

Never mistake a mission with how to go about accomplishing that mission because if the mission is forgotten, then, in this example, you might end up driving your car to Minneapolis. If you have defined your mission as "driving your car", then you would mistakenly believe that you had successfully completed your mission. However, your boss will disagree and your boss will be right. Sure, you did a great job driving your car, but you failed to complete the mission you were assigned, getting to Chicago.

In no way does this imply that ensuring that a business's computer and technology systems work is a bad thing. In fact, it is a very good thing for an IT department to be concerned with, but it is not the mission of IT. And neither is…

IT MYTH #2

IT's mission is to keep up with technology

This is false for similar reasons as discussed above. And again, let's be clear, yes, it is generally a good idea to keep up with technology. But, keeping up with technology is by no means the mission of IT. In fact, in some circumstances, keeping up with technology is not a good idea at all (more on that later).

There is another aspect of this myth that deserves further exploration because I believe that it is a fundamental ill within IT. And that aspect boils down to entitlement. Many IT departments and staff feel that they are in some way entitled to explore the latest and greatest technology, get trained on that technology and implement that technology.

This sense of entitlement comes from many things but is primarily driven by a desire to stay current and relevant within the IT market. The IT market moves and changes so fast that unless one has experience with the latest and greatest technology, the value of one's skills in that market is significantly diminished. Therefore, individuals who are career-minded will do everything in their power to become skilled in the latest technology. While this is certainly understandable, these individuals often give little consideration to the needs of a business as a whole, effectively placing their own needs and goals ahead of their business's needs and goals.

Let's face it; there are many businesses that can do everything they need to do on "legacy" technology. And when I say "legacy", this may refer to technology that is barely a year or two old. Unless IT departments and individuals understand their true mission, the fact that the latest and greatest technology may add very little, if any, value to a business can become lost.

The end result of this myth is that IT implements technology for the sake of technology and not for the sake of a business. This is a mistake that must be avoided at all costs. And that also goes for…

IT MYTH #3

IT's mission is to select, implement and support the best/right technology for a business

This is starting to get closer to the true mission of IT, but still fundamentally misses the true point and purpose of IT's mission. That is not to say that selecting, implementing and supporting the best/right technology for a business is not an admirable goal, but this is an end result of IT's true mission, not the mission itself.

The problem is one of how IT can judge what is the best/right technology for a business. Resolving this is issue falls back to the single, universal and undeniable mission of IT, which is…

THE SINGLE, UNIVERSAL AND UNDENIABLE MISSION OF IT

So, now that we have examined what IT's mission is not, we are left with answering the original question, "What is IT's mission within a business?" And contrary to what many might believe, there really is a single, universal and undeniable mission for IT, which is:

The mission of IT within a business is to make that business operate more efficiently, effectively and PROFITABLY.

But why is it so important for IT to understand and embrace this mission? Simple. Unless technology helps a business operate more profitably, why would any business implement that technology? Going back to the first canon of IT, "IT must make economic sense". This canon is number one for a reason. Unless an IT initiative makes economic sense, then there is no reason under the sun that the initiative should be undertaken. Hence, IT initiatives that are not fundamentally designed to make a business more profitable should never be undertaken.

Now, how can I be so certain that most IT departments and businesses do not understand this single, universal and undeniable mission of IT? Simple. Most businesses view IT as a cost center, not a profit center. Viewing IT as a cost center is proof positive that the single, universal and undeniable mission of IT has become lost. If businesses and IT departments truly understood the single, universal and undeniable mission of IT, IT departments would be viewed as profit centers, not cost centers.

Traditionally, a profit center is a department within a business that makes money and a cost center is one that spends money. Because IT hardware and software costs money, businesses tend to view IT as a cost center. But, remember the spreadsheet example. While the computer and software cost money (cost center), the net overall effect was that the business saved money (profit center). When an IT department follows the single, universal and undeniable mission of IT, the net overall effect will be that the IT department makes a business more profitable by reducing the time, money and effort required to make a business function.

Thus, IT must never be thought of as a single, isolated department within a business, but rather as a multifaceted, integral profit driver that can be leveraged within a business to increase efficiency, effectiveness and profitability. If IT is viewed in isolation, its net, positive effect on the rest of a business is lost. When this net, positive effect is lost, decisions regarding IT are made from the viewpoint of IT as a cost center. And if a business makes decisions about IT based on the false premise that IT is a cost center, then those decisions are likely to be wrong!

In this book I will do nothing less than show the reader how to transform an IT department from a cost center to a profit center. But in order to do this, we must first explore the very nature of business and IT's role within it.

2

What Is A Business?

A BUSINESS IS A PROCESS AND YOUR PROCESS IS YOUR BUSINESS

As one might expect, the answer to the question posed in the chapter title is encapsulated within the catchy chapter subtitle. Although it may not appear so at the time, this catchy phrase is actually more than just a catchy phrase. In fact, I believe that this simple phrase holds the key to running a business efficiently, effectively and most important, profitably.

A BUSINESS IS A PROCESS...

However, I am certain that there are those skeptics out there that need further proof than the mildly cryptic answer provided in the catchy subtitle. Therefore, I will elaborate by breaking down the answer into its two parts. The first, "A business is a process" answers the question literally although it might more accurately be phrased as "A business is a group of processes acting together as a collective process". But that's not as catchy.

But what do we mean when we talk about process? A process, simply stated, is a series of actions or operations that leads to an end. So let's think about how this definition applies to a business. Businesses sell things. Is sales a process? Well, in order to sell, one must prospect, qualify and close. That's a process. Manufacturing is also a process. Raw materials are run through particular operations in order to create a product. Research and Development (R&D) is a process. Marketing is a process. Delivery is a process. Billing is a process. Everything that a business does is a process. All of these individual processes are necessary for a business to function and the business itself is a collection of these processes as products and

5

services move from R&D to marketing to selling to manufacturing/delivery, to billing and finally to collection.

R&D -> Market -> Sell -> Manufacture/Deliver -> Bill -> Collect

This is a pretty simple, high-level process that describes all businesses. A business develops a product or service, markets it, sells it to interested parties, manufactures and delivers the goods and/or services, bills customers and collects compensation. Departments or divisions within companies are typically responsible for each component of this high-level process. But each of these process components can be further broken down into their own individual processes until one reaches the level of individuals within the business. Each individual within a business performs a series of repeated steps to accomplish their job. Therefore, this process view of a business applies equally well to an entire company, as well as each individual working for a company. All perform processes in order to function as a business.

So if a business is a process, or more accurately, a collection of processes, what about the mantra of people being the most important component of a business. If this were true, then would it not also stand to reason that people are what comprise a business, not process? Absolutely not. Getting a group of people together does not a business make. One can get a group of people together, but if they are not doing anything, it is not a business. To be a business, they need to be doing something. What are they doing? They are performing processes!

Therefore, any business can be implicitly modeled as the most basic type of system, one involving inputs, work (processes) and outputs. Depending on how one wishes to study the system one can either model the system as a closed system encompassing all three components or model the system as a control volume, focusing only on the process component. Either model is a valid way of looking at a business. For this analysis, a control volume will be used in order to focus on process. A basic control volume diagram is shown below:

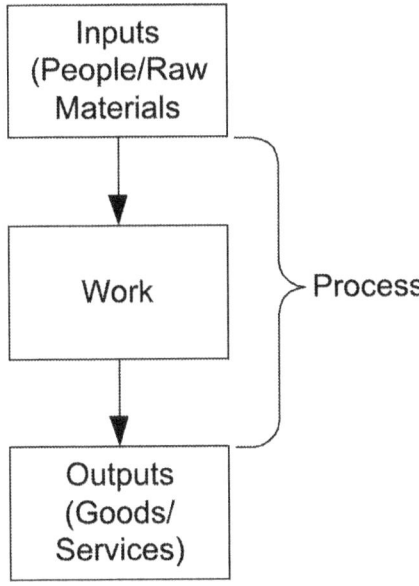

Figure 1: Basic Control Volume

I am certain that there may be some objections raised by equating people to raw materials, but no insult is intended. People are a crucial component of all businesses and no disrespect is intended. The reference is simply an end result of focusing on process and used to make a point. Even if a process is broken down to its smallest components of individuals directly performing tasks, each of those tasks can be broken down further into the exact process that individual executes to accomplish a task. Therefore, the individual is simply a contributor (input) to the process or action.

It is the fact that a business's employees know and understand how to execute the required processes that make them invaluable to a business, not the intrinsic value of the people themselves, no matter how intelligent or congenial. Make no mistake; having good people is critically important to a business because in most businesses, it is people that determine whether a business's processes work efficiently, effectively and accurately every time. In the majority of businesses, the better the people, the more efficiently, effectively and accurately the processes and as a consequence, the more efficient, effective and profitable the business.

In a truly free market economy, the most efficient, effective and profitable a business is, the better that business should do in the market. Now, nobody lives in a true free market economy, but even so, can it hurt to have one's internal business processes be as efficient, effective and economic as possible? It may not guarantee success, but doing these things better than one's competitors and for less money is a definitive leg up on the competition.

...YOUR PROCESS IS YOUR BUSINESS

This brings us to the second part of our catchy phrase, "your process is your business". What does this mean? ***This means that your core competency as a business is your business processes.*** One can improve a business by focusing on a business's processes and making them as efficient as possible. To state it a different way, one's true business as a company is its business's processes. Business processes are what define a company as a truly original and individual organization. Businesses that grasp the concept that the goods and services they sell are not really what their business is all about but instead simply inputs and outputs within their business processes are able to more effectively focus their abilities to deliver better, less expensive goods and services to their customers and out perform their competition.

3

An Introduction to Process

Regardless of just how important process is to a business, a business is comprised of more than just processes. The components that comprise a business are **People**, **Process** and **Tools** (Technology). When these three components are integrated and support one another, a business runs efficiently and effectively. When these components are not integrated, a business runs inefficiently and ineffectively.

PEOPLE, PROCESS AND TOOLS

In order for a business to be most effective and successful, all three components are necessary and important. However, process is the most overlooked component of the three. Companies spend a lot of time and resources on people and technology, as evidenced by the fact that every company has a Human Resources (HR) department and an IT department. So where is the Process Department? It does not exist because businesses fundamentally do not focus on the most important aspect of their business, their business processes!

But what about all of the standard departments within a business such as R&D, Marketing, Sales, Manufacturing/Delivery, Billing, etc? These departments are each responsible for major, macro-level processes within a business so is it not reasonable to expect that they are also responsible for process improvement within their segment of a business? Perhaps, in a perfect world, this would be the case. Unfortunately, in the real world, these departments are typically busy enough just trying to execute their daily processes, let alone improve upon them.

While businesses make regular investments in People and Tools to improve their efficiency and effectiveness, they rarely make investments in improving Process. And even in businesses that grasp the concept of process, those businesses generally fail to extend that concept to all facets of their business. Businesses like manufacturers and fast food chains have embraced their core business processes and spend large amounts of money and time building processes based around the manufacturing of a specific widget or the preparation of a particular food item. However, this leaves a huge number of other business processes such as administration, billing, sales, accounting, inventory, etc. that are almost never looked at or improved.

It is unfortunate that most businesses do not pay particular attention to their business processes because Process is the linchpin that ties people and technology into a cohesive business whole. To illustrate this point, think of a business as three concentric circles:

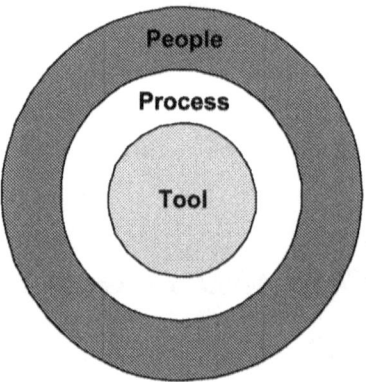

Figure 2: People, Process, Tool

People execute a process and technology ("Tool" in the diagram) assists people in supporting and automating that process. Process is a linchpin because without Process, people are either milling about randomly or using technology directly. Using technology directly is generally referred to as "Playing Solitaire" or "Web Browsing" or a host of other non-business related activities. Without Process, People and Tool cannot function as a cohesive business. It is Process that defines what a business is and does.

PROCESS INDEPENDENCE

But most companies do not focus on process; they focus on people. Some companies, however, have substituted good processes for good people. A prime example is the fast food industry. Let's face it; fast food chains are not hiring the most highly skilled people. Their primary employee pool mainly stems from high school students and other relatively unskilled laborers. Therefore, major fast food chains have very specific processes for the preparation of their food. This ensures that the food tastes the same regardless of where it is served. So, when you go to a *McDonalds* in Ohio and order a *Big Mac*, it tastes the same as when you go to a *McDonalds* in California and order a *Big Mac*. Unless of course they do not follow the process and do not caramelize the bun; I hate that.

So what does this mean? What this means is that people and process are independent of one another. One does not have to have good people in order to have good processes. This is simply the way most businesses work; they need to have good people in order to have good processes. But fast food chains and manufacturing facilities intrinsically prove that businesses can substitute good processes for good (highly skilled) people.

And if people and process are independent of one another, it also follows that good people do not automatically create good processes. Having a good worker that shows up to work on time and does his or her job sufficiently does not mean that such a worker creates good processes that allow him or her to do his or her job efficiently. That worker will create a process for getting his or her work done, but that process may not be the most efficient, effective or economic.

Furthermore, this independence between process and people means that good processes can be taught to "bad" or unskilled people. It is not necessary for the people themselves to come up with a process. Once a process is created, it can be taught to someone that knows nothing about the process as a whole, just his or her individual role in the process. This concept may seem obvious, but it is a key component in understanding how to attack the process problem as well a key cause of process degradation.

PROCESS ENTROPY

So why focus on process? If a business runs because of its processes, then shouldn't we expect those processes to evolve, grow and become more efficient as the company grows and matures? Sadly, no. While this may seem intrinsically logical, or at least hopeful, there are too many factors working against process within most businesses.

First, most people are task people, not process people. People tend to think in terms of tasks. People have tasks to accomplish certain things such as making a phone call, visiting a client, billing a client, etc. However, every task can be broken down into a process. Even a simple task such as making a phone call can be broken down into individual process steps such as looking up the phone number, dialing the phone, making an introduction, etc. We have been taught to think in terms of tasks from years of "highly intelligent habits" and other distressingly popular management babble.

In addition, the way in which people are employed discourages process efficiency. People are generally paid by the hour, not by how much they accomplish. The natural tendency of most individuals who are paid hourly is to do their work and go home at the end of the day. Most individuals are not particularly interested in just how efficient their work is. They may take pride in their work and perform their work well, but this does not mean that the processes they use to accomplish their work are efficient. Good people may have bad processes. And even if they have good processes, do they have great processes?

Furthermore, if we look at the nature of tasks, tasks generally require inputs and outputs. Because the people executing these tasks only make up a small portion of a business, the inputs and outputs of these tasks generally involve other people. This lends another element to the process puzzle. Even if most employees of a business have great processes, all it takes is for a couple of employees to have bad processes to have a serious, detrimental impact on the entire business because those employees with bad processes become bottlenecks within the overall processes of the business. Unless these interactions between employees are studied, defined and made efficient, individuals within a business must discover on their own the most efficient, or at the very least, sufficient, way of working with one another. This instinct to find a sufficient way of working together, not an efficient way of working together, can be a huge cause of process inefficiency.

Finally, tasks are learned behavior for most employees. Someone, at some point in time defined a process used to complete a particular task. That process was probably never written down and simply handed down to others. What's more, a particular employee's tasks are only a small component within a larger process and so individuals within a business are generally only familiar with their specific components and not an entire process. Unless a process is continually improved upon and someone analyzes the entire process, the individual parts of a process start to break down over time as people, processes and tools change. This slow change is equivalent to the "grapevine" game of telling a story to one person, who then tells the story to someone else, who tells the story to someone else, etc. At the end of the grapevine, the story is completely different. Processes evolve, or more specifically degrade, similarly. Think of the original story in a rumor as the original, perfectly efficient process. Now think of changes to that story as caused by inefficient storytelling. Small inconsistencies and inefficiencies within the individual processes impact the efficiency of the entire process to a much greater extent than the simple sum of the inefficiencies. In a grapevine, the entire meaning of a rumor or story will change and similarly, in a business, the entire reason for a particular process may change or even become non-existent over time.

Therefore, there are multiple factors working against process efficiency in companies. All of these factors slowly work to degrade processes over time. This slow degradation is referred to as **Process Entropy**. Entropy is a concept borrowed from science and refers to the loss of energy within a system due to things like friction and other environmental factors. This entropy is constantly working against good process efficiency, as small inefficiencies slowly become very big inefficiencies. Unfortunately, there are typically very few forces working for process efficiency and combating process entropy.

To be successful, businesses must change the dynamic within their company of the forces working for and against good processes. Changing this dynamic requires all components; the People, Processes and Tools, of a business to change. Good processes do not simply happen. Developing good processes takes a fair amount of effort and it takes additional effort to keep processes up-to-date. Processes should be constantly improved upon and grow with a company. But this does not always happen. In fact, it almost never happens. People learn a way of doing things and continue to execute a process that way without ever really thinking about the actual process or how they might do things more efficiently.

PROCESS AND IT

Now where this ties into IT is that when IT burst onto the business scene in 1980, nobody focused on *SuperCalc*, the software, or the business process problem of manual recalculation that was solved. What did they focus on? They focused on the Tool, the computer, in many respects the least relevant component. From this time forward, the entire computer industry was now Tool focused and the mentality developed that these Tools, computers and digital systems, could be sprinkled around like "pixie dust" in order to solve business problems. This is simply not the case. In fact, computers really can cause more problems than they solve if used inappropriately. If one automates a bad business process, all one has accomplished is making a bad business process happen really, really fast. That solves nothing.

So, after decades of being told how much personal computers and digital systems will automate and improve our businesses and our lives by increasing productivity and decreasing manual labor, today, many argue that computers have accomplished very little or none of this. Many organizations still have too much manual work, are forced to work long hours and often the computer systems seem to create more problems than they solve. Add to this various statistics estimating that 74% of all IT projects fail, and some are left to wonder why computers and digital technology have failed to deliver on the promises of greater productivity, greater automation, less manual labor and ultimately greater profits for individuals and businesses.

Now, I believe that much of this attitude comes from people forgetting what life was like before computers. To be fair, computers have provided great advances in automation and productivity. However, IT within business has failed in a number of ways to deliver its full potential to businesses. The reason for this is actually quite simple. Computers are a tool, like a hammer or screwdriver or any other tool. Now, computers are a very flexible and powerful tool, but they are still just like any other tool. That is, a tool is not a solution for anything; it is simply a tool that provides one component or a means of arriving at a solution. The key component that is missing when people talk about solving a business problem is Process. Most companies understand People and understand Tools but miss Process. But Process is the key to everything within a business because as we have seen, everything in a business is a process.

The fundamental reason why process is often completely overlooked is because process generally does not have a physical manifestation. Process is the least visible and therefore the least understood of the three components of a business. But the concept of process is not that difficult. More reliable, accurate and efficient processes mean that a business is accomplishing more with less which means that a business is more effective and efficient, which means a business is more profitable. Achieving this result is what I refer to as ***Process Profitability***.

4

Process Profitability

Given a choice between investing in People, Process or Tools, businesses invariably short shrift process because it is so often overlooked. However, because a business is really just a collection of processes, investments in process pay substantial dividends over and above investments in just Tools or People. This is because investments in Process affect all three components of a business; People, Process and Tools, while investments in Tools or People only affect one component of a business. In addition, by investing in process, one is truly investing in one's business because *a business is a process and your process is your business.*

By investing the time and money to improve and automate business processes, corporations can achieve **Process Profitability**, or increased profitability through highly efficient and effective business processes. To see how this can be accomplished, we must delve further into the world of process and process efficiency.

PROCESS EFFICIENCY

When a business and an individual perform a process, they are expending Time in order to accomplish Work. In a perfect world, every second of the time spent on a job would be spent accomplishing work for a business. If this were the case, the people and their business would operate at 100% efficiency, meaning that every unit of time produced one unit of useful work. And we could graph this relationship between time and work as follows:

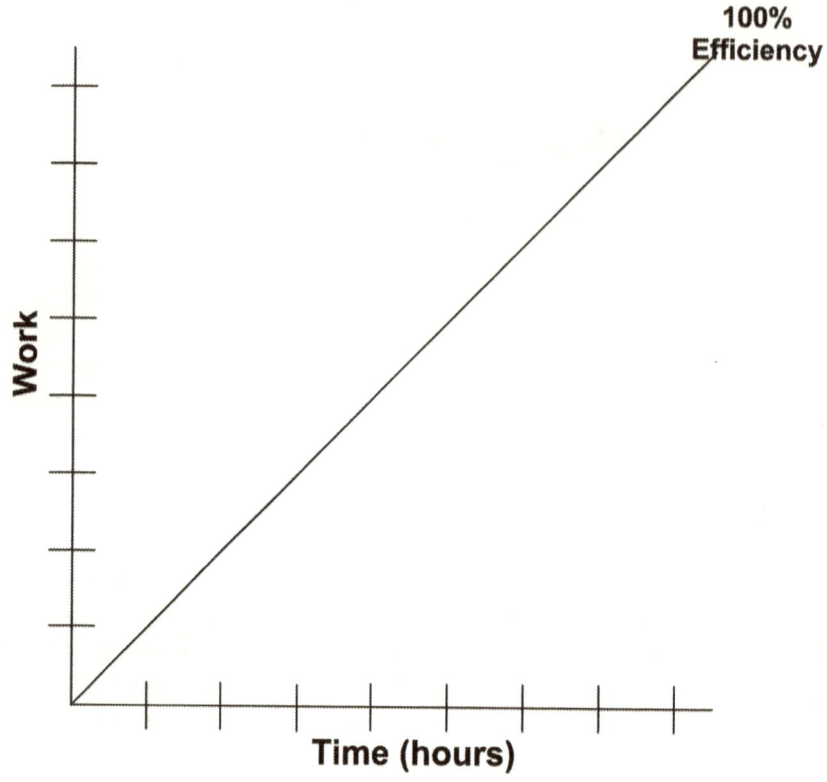

Figure 3: 100% Efficiency

As one can see from the graph, if one unit of time equals one unit of work, then a 45-degree line represents 100% efficiency.

Now, if we were to use this same graph and apply it to a business, we could average out the time and work output of each individual within a business and come up with an average amount of work produced by employees within a given amount of time. This might look something like the following diagram.

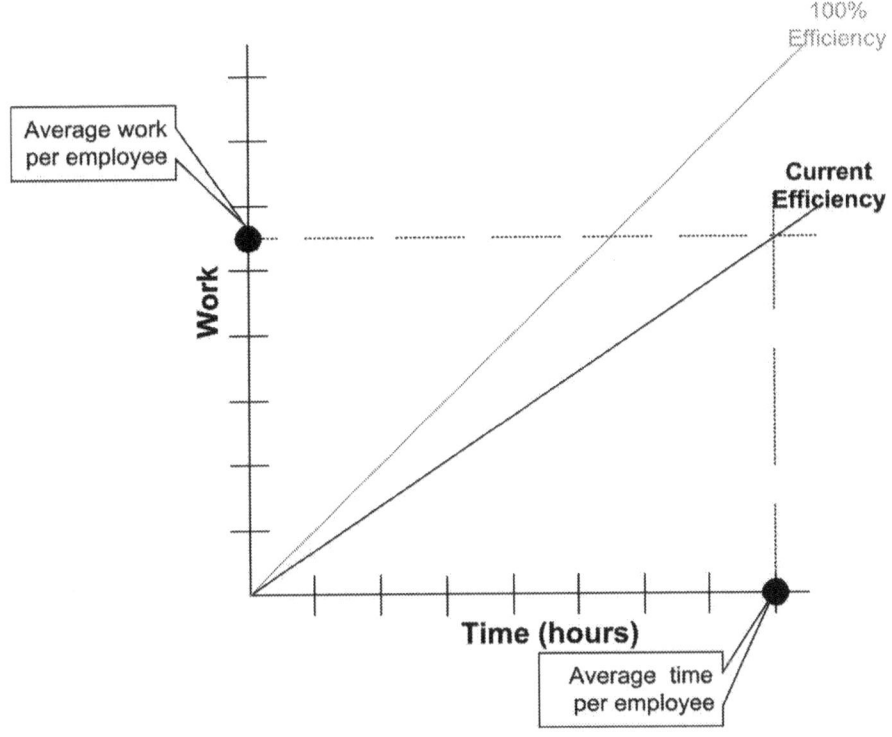

Figure 4: Average efficiency

Because we are currently talking about abstract concepts of "work units", we cannot use exact numbers for the work output and efficiency of our fictitious business. However, one can see from the graph that the Current Efficiency of the business will be less than the theoretical maximum efficiency of 100% due to things like vacation, sick leave, coffee breaks, etc.

Of course the goal for any employer is to accomplish the most amount of work in the least amount of time (cost). But, businesses have some odd ways of going about it. Some make their employees work overtime. But simply working more does not increase efficiency. In fact, working extra hours generally breeds poor performance or decreased efficiency. So, one is actually paying more per unit of work output to get the extra work accomplished even if a business does not have to pay increased wages for overtime work. If a business does have to pay extra (time and a half) for overtime work, then that business is really paying a high price tag for that extra work. Therefore, the trick to making a business more efficient and hence more profitable is not to heap on more work or additional hours, but to instead change the slope of its efficiency graph. But exactly how can this be accomplished?

A MATTER OF TIME

In order to answer that question, we must first look a little deeper into the Time axis of the graph. The Time axis of the graph is actually composed of two components, **Unproductive Time** and **Productive Time**. That is to say, employees of a business are either producing work or not. Unproductive Time is the time that employees spend going to the bathroom, eating lunch, taking vacation, taking personal phone calls, etc.

A typical management strategy to squeeze more work out of employees is to try to cut down on the amount of this Unproductive Time. However, there is a maximum to how much Unproductive Time can be cut and as deeper cuts are made, employers typically lose employees to burn-out, job dissatisfaction, etc. Morale suffers, efficiency goes down and a business may actually lose ground rather than gain ground. Not so good.

So, let's take a closer look at Productive Time. This is the time spent by employees performing Processes that produce Work. This time is almost never considered by employers because the employees are being productive, which is a good thing, so why mess with a good thing? But why not take a look at Productive Time? If no one pays attention to Productive Time, then it is very likely that this Productive Time is not really all that productive in terms of efficiency. Good processes do not happen by accident and poor processes are a huge drain on efficiency. So, let's ignore Unproductive Time and focus solely on Productive Time because Productive Time is the only component of time that actually produces work and can therefore impact our efficiency curve.

So what if we could improve the efficiency of the processes that a person performs? And let's be conservative and say that we will look for just a five percent (5%) efficiency gain, meaning that the Work performed during Productive Time is accomplished five percent 5% faster. 5% of an average eight 8 hour day is twenty-four (24) minutes, so we will round this to thirty (30) minutes or half-an-hour. This graph would look like the following:

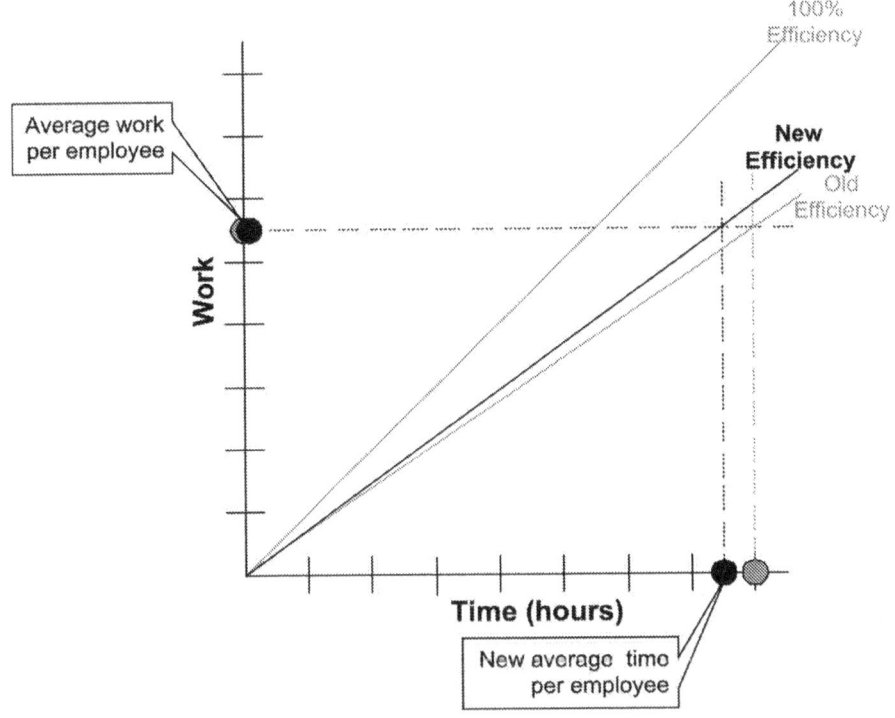

Figure 5: Adjusted average efficiency

If one improves the efficiency of Productive Time such that 30 minutes can be shaved off of the time required of an employee to accomplish a specific task or set of tasks, the efficiency curve shifts upward closer to 100% efficiency. If we extrapolate upon this and can find a way to make every employee 5% more efficient, then the average time per employee will be reduced by 30 minutes. The amount of Work accomplished will be the same but the efficiency of the employees and the business as a whole has increased by 5%.

So what does this mean, a 5% efficiency gain? A typical way of looking at this is that a 5% efficiency gain means that a business does not need 5% of its work force. This is a perfectly valid way of looking at things, but it is perhaps not the best way. To prove the point, let's introduce a specific example.

Let's take a typical two hundred (200) seat business with an average annual employee adjusted gross salary of $30,000 and an average annual revenue per employee of $100,000. 5% of 200 is ten (10). Therefore, if this business can operate 5% more efficiently, it could theoretically cut 10 people. If this business cut 10 people, it would save $300,000 annually ($30,000 * 10). This is definitely not chump change, especially since that $300,000 is pure profit because the same amount of work is being accomplished with a reduced cost structure.

ENERGY

But, what if there was a way to make even more profit from a 5% efficiency gain? In order to show this I need to introduce one final concept, Energy. Let's show this on our graph.

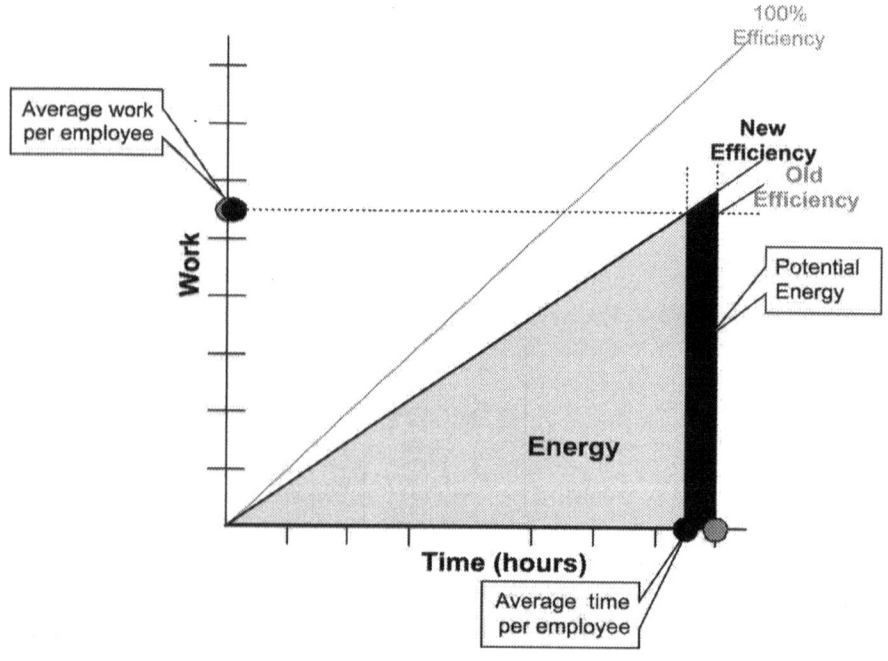

Figure 6: Energy

Now, I won't bore you with the Calculus involved, but suffice to say that the area under the efficiency curve is the Energy expended by a business in order to accomplish the Work in the given Time. However, please note the black, shaded portion of the graph. This portion represents the **Potential Energy** of the business.

By making efficiency improvements, we effectively gave employees back 30 minutes of their day. But, if a business could take advantage of those 30 minutes to perform more Work at the same Efficiency, then it could do 5% more Work in the same time period. This is important because the potential to do 5% more work means that a business can generate 5% more revenue with the exact same cost structure.

So, let's go back to our example 200-person business with an average annual revenue per employee of $100,000. These figures mean that our example business's annual revenue is $20 million (200 * $100,000). 5% of $20 million is $1 million. Therefore, if we take that 5% efficiency gain and find a way to use that potential energy to generate 5% more revenue, our example business can make $1 million more per year. This is over three times the profit that would be generated by cutting 10 people with an average annual salary of $30,000 each. Therefore, it is far more profitable to make employees more efficient and then to find a way to utilize that time to generate additional revenue versus cutting one's work force.

To summarize, businesses can improve their profitability by focusing on Process, not Tools or People. In fact, it is imperative that the Process issue be attacked first, before selecting or building a Tool to further improve the Process. Once the Process is understood, well documented and efficient, then Tools (computers and digital systems) can be brought in to automate the process and further improve efficiency. By focusing on Process, businesses can improve profitability by increasing the efficiency of their business processes. This approach is called ***Process Profitability*** and achieving Process Profitability is an essential first step in becoming a highly efficient, effective and profitable business.

5

Capturing the Ability to Learn

Now that I have shown how improvements in business processes lead to greater business profits, or Process Profitability, the next obvious task is to figure out exactly how to observe and improve business processes. To accomplish this feat, a business must develop the ability to learn. Unfortunately, this is easier said than done.

MEMORY AND LEARNING

It is fundamentally understood that all individuals have the ability to learn. This ability to learn comes from a single capability of the brain, memory. Our brains take input from their five senses and can remember a portion of the information that they take in from these senses. Without memory, we would not be able to learn anything. If we could not remember the sounds and motions to form letters, syllables and words we would not even be able to speak a common language.

Because individuals can remember past events, even if only subconsciously, individuals learn things all the time. This ability to learn pervades every individual as well as, collectively, society as a whole and has led to truly wonderful inventions and progress. But what is truly wonderful about our ability to learn is that we do not even need to specifically think about remembering or learning anything. In fact, what we experience through our senses alone provides constant education. Our brains seem to have a will of their own in regards to their capability to remember and learn, often to the chagrin of many people whose brains might refuse to bend to their will.

This intrinsic ability to learn is what allows individuals to develop specialized skills that become valuable assets to corporations. However, corporations themselves, while treated as living entities in many respects and fundamentally composed of individuals, have no intrinsic ability to remember past events. Because of this lack of ability to remember, corporations have no ability to learn by themselves. This means that unless energy is expended specifically to build a memory for a corporation, a business might never get better at what it does.

This is why people are so important to a business. In most businesses, people are used to simulate memory. Although corporations have no intrinsic means of building memory, the individuals that work for corporations do. Therefore, if a business retains the individuals that comprise it, a business retains memory of past events.

These individual memories of employees within a corporation arise from those individuals performing business processes. The repetition of these processes allows individuals to learn their jobs and, in effect, learn what a business does. These individual memories form a collection of memories referred to as a **Collective Memory**.

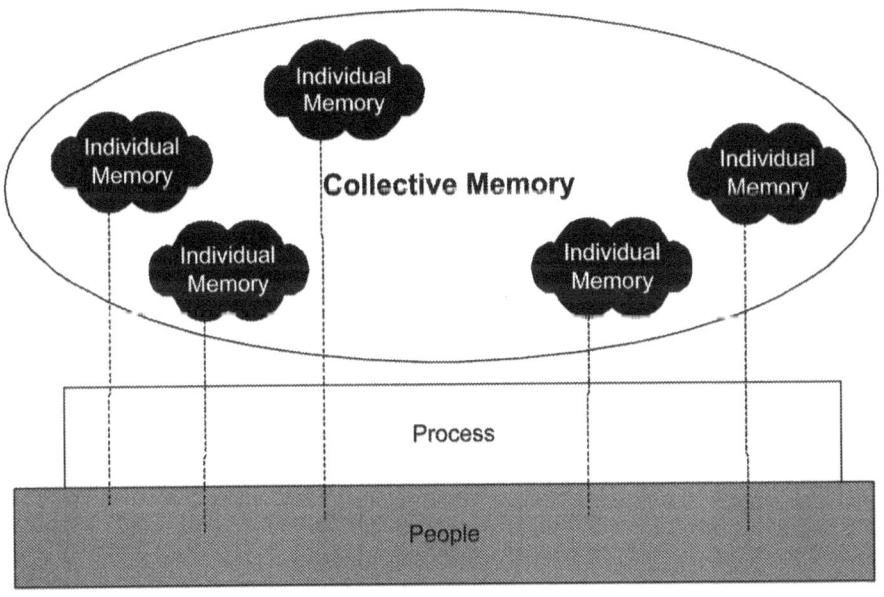

Figure 7: Collective Memory

COLLECTIVE MEMORY

The problem with collective memory is that it is comprised of the shared individual memories of all of the employees within a corporation. Therefore, when an individual leaves a business, a portion of that collective memory is permanently lost. This is because human memory and the ability to recall and relate memories are imperfect. An individual leaving a business may impart some of his or her knowledge of past events, memories, to successors but this transfer of knowledge is always going to be imperfect. Therefore, businesses always lose collective memory when individuals leave.

As long as the rate and relative magnitude of collective memory loss remains low, the impact to a business is tolerable. However, relearning information is never a trivial or inexpensive proposition and this is why businesses suffer when they lose individuals. Turnover within a business costs time and money in terms of retraining and reintegration. New individuals must relearn processes and integrate with the collective memory of their business.

This reliance on collective memory has an even more insidious cost to businesses. As collective memory is slowly lost, corporations forget why they do things. This is the result of imperfect training when hiring a new individual, the grapevine effect if you will. Training generally focuses on "How" to do things, not "Why" those things are done. As processes become more complex and involve more individuals, this problem becomes rampant because each individual only knows how to perform his or her individual part of a process. Compound this with the fact that each individual probably only has a vague understanding of an entire process and it is easy to see how process degradation can grow exponentially within a business.

I am reminded of a joke that circulated in email spam about five gorillas in a cage. Five gorillas are placed in a cage along with a bunch of bananas at the other end of the cage. Every time a gorilla traveled past the halfway mark in the room between the gorillas and bananas, fire hoses would be used to spray down the gorillas and keep them from the bananas. Pretty soon, the gorillas did not go after the bananas. Then, one of the original gorillas is pulled out of the room and a new gorilla placed into the room. This new gorilla immediately makes a move toward the bananas but is attacked and beaten by the four original gorillas in order to make sure that they are not sprayed by the fire hoses. One-by-one, all of the original gorillas are replaced by new gorillas and even once all of the original gorillas are gone and the fire hoses permanently turned off, the gorillas never go after the bananas and any new gorillas introduced into the cage who make a run at the bananas are soundly pummeled.

The point of the joke is that this is the model of how corporate policy is created. "This is the way we do things because this is the way we have always done things." The scary part of the joke is that it is dead-on with regards to business processes. This is exactly how poor processes develop. There may have been some very good reasons for a particular process when that process was created, but over time the reasons for that process may change or become nonexistent. Thus, people forget why they do things, even if they remember how to do things. And this is a direct result of relying on collective memory. Over time, the why's and how's of a process change, but there is no one left that understands the entire process and thus inefficiencies creep in, or in many cases race in like a sprinter running the 100 yard dash. This is a major cause of Process Entropy and over time, process entropy can seriously impact the overall efficiency and profitability of a corporation.

CORPORATE MEMORY

So, how does a business solve this problem? First, we must recognize the failings of collective memory and propose an alternate solution. That alternate solution is **Corporate Memory**. Corporate memory is knowledge of past events retained by a business and not by any single individual or group of individuals. Now, because a business has no brain to automatically records past events, a business must attempt to simulate the human brain. Before, we discuss how this can be accomplished, let's look at a simple model for Corporate Memory.

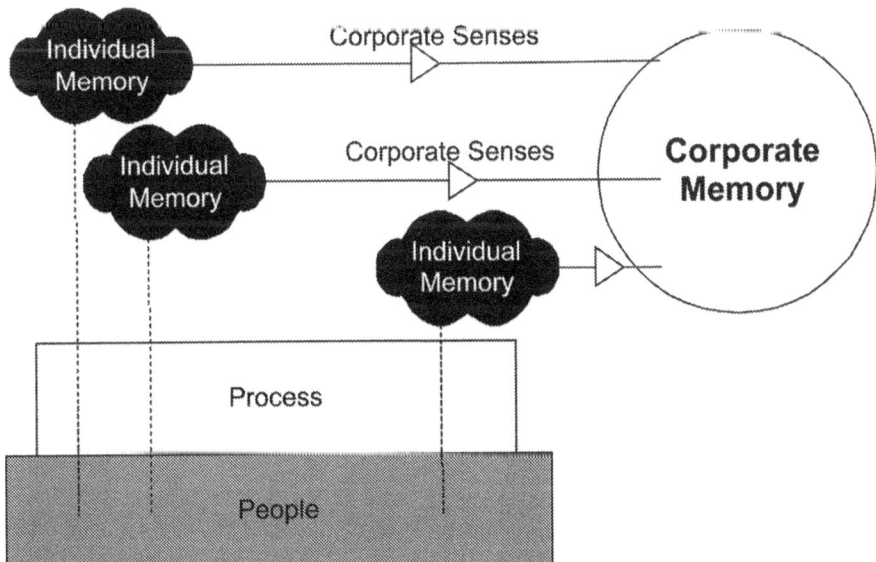

Figure 8: Corporate Memory

Two important components should be noted in the diagram. First, unlike collective memory, which is composed of the individual memories of employees, Corporate Memory exists as a distinct entity, completely separate from the memories of individuals. Second, because Corporate Memory is a distinct entity, and because businesses have no innate ability to learn, there must be some mechanism or process put into place that captures this Corporate Memory. This transfer mechanism is referred to as **Corporate Senses**. Just like human beings have five senses that allow them to observe the outside world, businesses must develop similar mechanisms. What we remember as individuals is really simply the information that our five senses collect and transfer to our brain. Therefore, it is imperative that businesses develop similar senses in order to learn.

But just exactly what are these Corporate Senses and how does one go about creating and using them to capture Corporate Memory? Well, first, we must define the exact nature of Corporate Memory. This is actually quite simple. In order to be considered Corporate Memory, information must be written down or otherwise permanently recorded as a piece of corporate property. Otherwise, this information is simply stuck in some individual's brain as individual and collective memory rather than Corporate Memory.

CORPORATE SENSES

Now, in terms of the actual mechanical transfer and creation of Corporate Memory, there are various ways of attacking this problem. The original diagram of Corporate Memory shown above shows a simplistic method of creating Corporate Memory. Essentially, each individual tries to organize and write down all that he or she knows about his or her job. This is a very simple method of capturing Corporate Memory, but it is by no means the best method.

The problems with this method are many but we will just note the two most important problems. First, a business using this method relies solely upon the potentially flawed memories of each individual as well as each individual's capability to organize and accurately disseminate the crucial information about his or her tasks. Second, this method of capturing corporate memory is a one-time, or at least infrequent, process and requires additional hours and effort by every individual within a business.

To find a better way of collecting and capturing Corporate Memory, let's look at how people collect and capture their individual memories and let's pay particularly attention to how individuals learn. To this end, the phrase "Practice makes perfect" comes to mind. While an obvious cliché, there is an element of truth in it. Human beings learn by practicing the same thing over and over and over again. This repetition of the same task builds up a memory of that task over time. The ingrained memory of that task is commonly referred to as learning.

Where o' where in a company can we look for tasks that are repeated over, and over and over again? Luckily, this question is extremely easy to answer. We simply need to look at the processes of a business because business processes are typically repeated ad infinitum. And since a business is a collection of processes that is itself a process, *"a business is a process"*, we can look at nearly any level and find a process that is repeated over and over and over again. A business Markets, Sells, Delivers, Bills and Collects, over and over and over again. The daily tasks of each individual within the business are generally repeated over and over and over again.

Therefore, if a business could somehow just "observe" and record these processes, it would collect Corporate Memory that could then be used for learning. This, then, is where we should focus our Corporate Senses, upon these business processes, both at a macroscopic (business unit/department) and microscopic (individual daily tasks) level. At each level, particular processes are continually repeated. Each repetition of the process is referred to as a cycle. This can be diagrammed as follows:

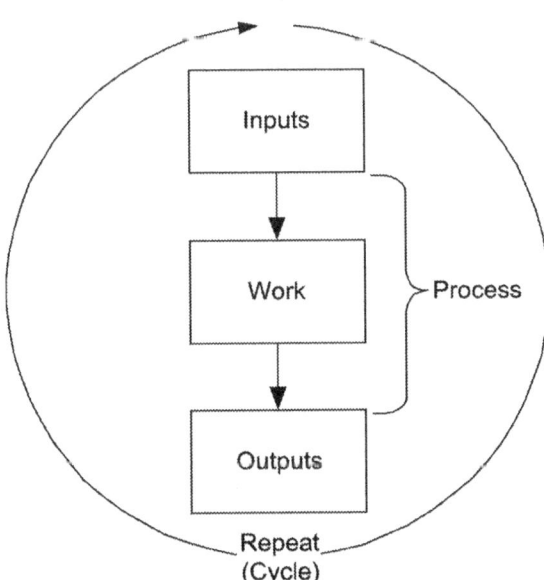

Figure 9: Process Cycle

Each cycle takes the same, equivalent, inputs, executes the same, equivalent, work and produces the same, equivalent, outputs. The specifics of the inputs and outputs might vary each time so we need to talk about equivalent inputs, outputs and work. Let's take a simple process as a demonstration.

Suppose we have as an input an unordered list of surnames and a desired output of an alphabetized list of those surnames. The actual names in the list may vary each time, but the equivalent input of "an unordered list of surnames", the work of sorting those names and the equivalent output of "an alphabetized list of surnames" never changes. Each execution of this process is a cycle. Because, by definition, a cycle is continually repeated, if we can observe or sense this cycle, we can collect large amounts of data or metrics about a process over time.

A good place to start when observing or sensing a cycle is to sense the inputs and outputs of the cycle as well as the time required for the work involved. This basic information can help a business learn a lot about a process. For example, let's take a typical Sales process and see how this concept might be used:

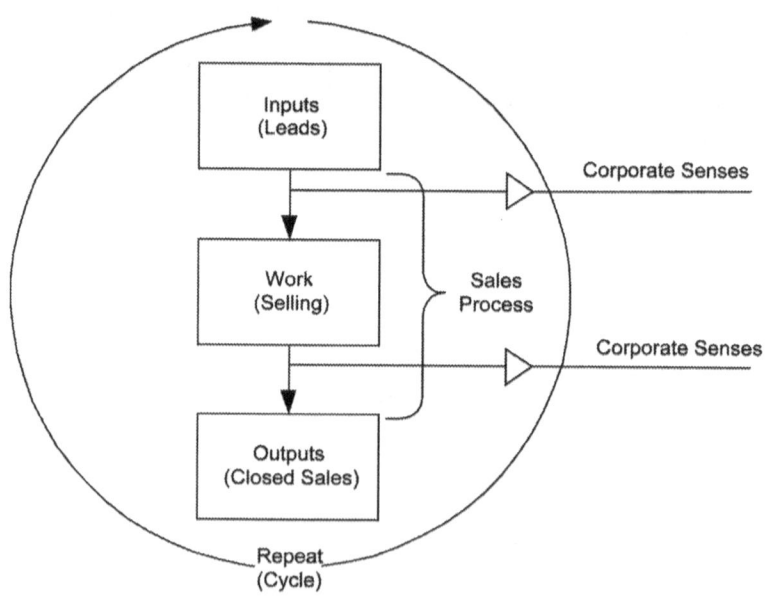

Figure 10: Corporate Senses

By sensing how many Leads come in and how many Closed Sales come out, a business can immediately begin to determine the effectiveness of its Sales process.

If one also tracks the time those leads come in and the time the sales close or are dropped, a business can also begin to determine the efficiency of its Sales process.

FEEDBACK

So now, building upon our basic control volume diagram, we have a method of analyzing and learning about any process within a business. But, in order to make process improvements, there is one final concept that must be introduced, Feedback. Up until now, we have focused on how to capture Corporate Memory in order to learn what a business does. This Corporate Memory serves as the basis for a business to learn. Now it is time to put that learning to use. This is accomplished through Feedback. Feedback is the process of taking corporate learning and disseminating that knowledge back to people and processes in order to improve a process as a whole. We can diagram Feedback as follows:

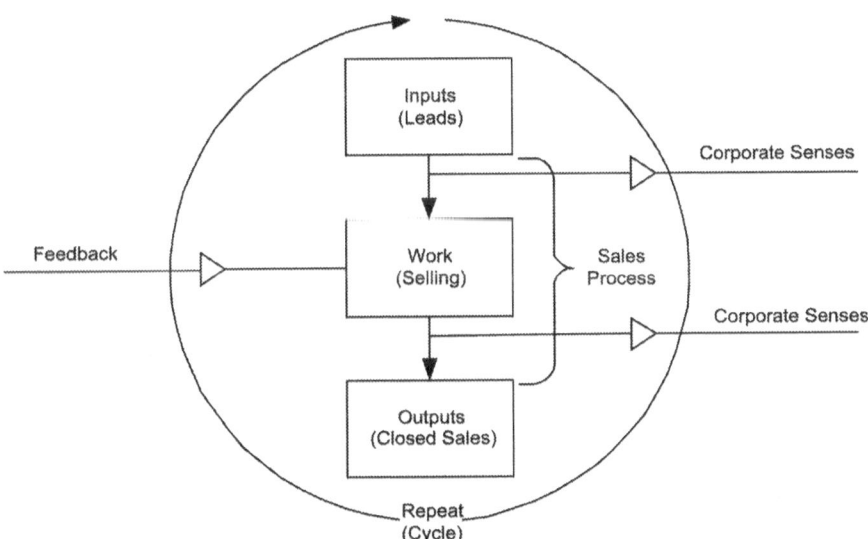

Figure 11: Feedback

Feedback closes the loop between Corporate Memory and the people and processes of a business. Applying Feedback changes a process, which; in turn, changes the information being recorded by Corporate Senses. These changes can then be monitored via Corporate Senses and compared with past data to demonstrate and prove whether the Feedback created a positive or negative influence.

The entire loop from Corporate Senses to Corporate Memory to Feedback becomes what is referred to as a Control System. An example of a common control system is the cruise control in a car. When setting the cruise control in a car, a computer monitors the speed of the car (Corporate Senses) and checks that against the speed that has been set (Corporate Memory). If the computer senses that the car is speeding up or slowing down, it provides information (Feedback) to the acceleration pedal to cause the car to either speed up or slow down in order to compensate and maintain the correct speed.

In summary, Corporate Memory is the documentation of business processes. By keeping a record of the processes and by storing data about these processes, a business builds Corporate Memory and gains two key advantages. First, Corporate Memory creates the ability for a business to learn and improve its business processes. Without Corporate Memory, there is no basis from which to learn new and better methods of doing things because there is no knowledge of the past. Second, Corporate Memory helps protect a business when losing people. People are key to a business because without Corporate Memory, they alone have the knowledge about a business's processes. Extracting this knowledge allows a business to protect itself from the loss of large amounts of knowledge about its business processes and reduces training costs associated with teaching new individuals how to perform its business processes.

6

Micro, Mezzo and Macro Processes

Improvements in business processes lead to greater business profits, Process Profitability. In order to improve business processes, businesses must observe and learn about their business processes. This is accomplished through Corporate Senses, Corporate Memory and Feedback. The next step is to determine where and how to improve business processes. To do this, we must first take a close look at process within all levels of a business.

There are nearly endless ways to break down individual levels within the full spectrum of a business's processes. Therefore, in order to simplify our analysis we will define three levels from which to analyze business processes, from a micro level, from a mezzo level and from a macro level. Micro level processes are those processes performed by an individual, mezzo level processes are those processes that span two or more individuals within a single business unit (intra-business unit) and macro level processes are those processes that span two or more business units (inter-business unit).

Most analysis of process within a business, if it occurs at all, occurs at the macro process level or the mezzo process level at a high level, such as an entire department or business unit. Process improvements at the micro level are generally left to the individuals performing the processes. The reasons for this focus on macro and mezzo processes are quite simple. First, macro and mezzo level processes are easier to grasp and observe. Second, macro and mezzo level processes can be analyzed and broken down without offending or singling out any particular individual. Third, macro and mezzo level processes are commonly, and often mistakenly, viewed as higher dollar items than micro or individual processes. And finally, most process improvement within business comes from business managers, who tend to take a top-down approach to analyzing a business. They think "big picture", which is what they have been trained to do.

Now, without question, there are process efficiency gains to be made at the macro and mezzo levels. However, even more efficiency gains can be made at the micro level. In addition, by analyzing processes at a micro level, one automatically makes gains in mezzo and macro level process efficiencies. The reason is quite simple. The micro processes that individuals perform daily ultimately make up the mezzo and macro level processes. By analyzing and improving micro-level processes, the mezzo and macro level processes come along for the ride. However, the converse is not true. One can improve mezzo and macro level processes but actually lose efficiency gains due to a detrimental impact at the micro-process level. Hence, by breaking down daily business processes and analyzing them at a micro-level, true efficiencies are gained because one understands the fundamental, daily tasks that comprise these business processes. This is done by breaking down the tasks that individuals perform into micro-processes. A micro-process is simply a typical task given to an individual such as filing records or mailing, etc. There is no task too trivial that it cannot be broken down into a micro-process. This micro-process can then be optimized to make it more efficient.

MICRO PROCESS EFFICIENCIES

Now, the discussion thus far has concentrated only on the time efficiency savings (process efficiency). However, there is also product efficiency, which is the efficient use of products within a business process. The efficient use of products can save large amounts of money as well. Office items such as pens, staples, Post-It Notes and other items can add up to significant cost savings. By breaking down tasks into micro-processes, a business can also analyze the use of supplies and make efficiency savings in this area as well.

Let's run through an example by taking what many might consider a relatively simple job, such as that of a phone operator or receptionist. If a business can improve the micro process efficiencies of a receptionist's job would it not stand to reason that a business could improve the process efficiencies of just about any job? Of course, so let's take a real world example of process and product efficiencies of a real phone operator job.

The following example is based upon a real phone operator's job for a 200-employee medical services firm based in Columbus, Ohio. The following table summarizes the process efficiencies and related product efficiencies made by a phone operator that has a particular knack for ferreting out process inefficiencies.

Time Efficiency Savings						
Process	Unit Saved	Units Saved	Time Period	Cost/ Unit	Savings/ Year	Notes
"Doing numbers"	Hour	1.5	Day	$10.00	$3,375.00	Process improvement
Report numbering for medical records	Hour	1	Day	$10.00	$2,250.00	Process improvement
Stuffing envelopes	Hour	1	Day	$10.00	$2,250.00	Process improvement
Faxing items for other people	Hour	1	Day	$2.00	$450.00	Operator's wage is about $2 less than others
Product Efficiency Savings						
Description	Unit Saved	Units Saved	Time Period	Cost/ Unit	Savings/ Year	Notes
Staples saved in outgoing reports	Staple	200	Week	$0.00055	$5.72	Process improvement
Postage saved by not using staples	Postage	60	Week	$0.23	$717.60	Staples add weight to postage
Use recycled paper instead of post-it notes	Post-it Notes Package	2	Week	$2.00	$208.00	Reuse of paper
Reuse extra paper printed by scheduling system	500/ream paper	1	Month	$10.00	$120.00	Reuse of paper
Recycling of paper clips	Paperclip	10	Day	$0.005	$11.25	Using existing paper clips
TOTAL					**$9,387.57**	

Table 1: Time Efficiency Savings

As one can see from the table, these process and product efficiencies save $9,387.57 per year, or over 30% of the phone operator's adjusted cost to the company of $31,200 per year (2080 hours per year * $10.00/hour * an overhead factor of 1.5). The Savings/Year column was calculated by taking the Units Saved and multiplying this with the number of Time Periods in a year (see table below). This product was then multiplied by the Cost/Unit to arrive at Savings/Year. So, looking at the first line of saving 1.5 hours in a day, multiplied by 225 working days per year at a cost per unit of $10/hour equals $3,375.00 (1.5 * 225 * $10).

Unit	Units in Year
Work Hours	1800
Total Hours (Work Hours, Vacation, Sick Leave, etc.)	2080
Day	225
Week	52
Month	12

Table 2: Time Periods

One of the other interesting items that one will notice in the first table is that the most significant cost savings came from "Process improvement". This means that our phone operator was trained on one way of doing things, the way things had always been done, and came up with a superior method of accomplishing the same tasks in a much shorter amount of time by changing and improving the processes of accomplishing those tasks.

As one can see, we can break down the individual tasks of each person into micro-processes and make them more efficient. Therefore, does it not also stand to reason that we could take tasks that span more than one individual and make those tasks more efficient in the same manner? Of course we can. Tasks that span multiple individuals within a business unit, mezzo processes, can also be made more efficient by improving the process as a whole and can be accomplished by many of the same methods. The same goes for macro processes. However, a true picture of one's business processes will only emerge by attacking the problem from a micro-level.

By making improvements to micro-processes, a side benefit is that a business generates a detailed picture of each employee's utilization. A typical business will have some individuals that are under utilized and others that are over utilized. If viewing this from a statistical perspective, the overall utilization and efficiency of people will roughly conform to a standard bell-shaped curve. Those that are over utilized are in danger of burn-out and those that are under utilized could be adding more value to the business. Note that over utilization and under utilization are not obvious signs of good or bad employees, it may simply mean that a business is supplying too much work to some employees and too little to others. By freeing up some of everyone's time, the opportunity exists to reshuffle the workload from those that have too much work. In addition, by identifying under utilized individuals, workload can again be shuffled to more evenly distribute the workload. Another benefit of focusing on micro-processes is that it can lead to still more savings through the building of Corporate Memory. By analyzing micro-processes and keeping a record of these processes, a business can build Corporate Memory and take advantage of its benefits.

By analyzing micro-processes a business can ensure that its employees are utilized effectively and have all of the processes within the company working as efficiently as possible. In addition, a business can build Corporate Memory to further teach it how to continue improving processes and insulate it from the loss of employees.

PROCESS EFFICIENCY AND IT

So where does IT come into the picture? First, focusing Corporate Senses on micro-process will generate a tremendous amount of data about those processes. This data should be collected automatically and placed within a system where it can be analyzed. This is a perfect application for computers and digital systems. Second, IT can give people the tools necessary to perform their jobs even more efficiently and effectively. Think of the process efficiencies, and hence profitability, that can be gained by applying IT to individual micro-processes. How much more efficiency could be gained by giving people the tools necessary to do their job even more efficiently, effectively and economically? This is the tools stage of business process efficiency. Once a business has the correct and most efficient processes, that business can automate and make its processes even more efficient through the use of computer systems and other tools. This further increases efficiency, which further increases profits.

7

Specialization

So now the question becomes, how can IT be used to help a business achieve Process Profitability by aiding in the creation of Corporate Memory and further improving business processes? This is the task that is tackled in the remainder of this book. However, in order to convince any skeptics that may believe that this is not even the job of IT, we need to take a look at a couple key process concepts, starting with **Specialization**.

My wife went to the doctor one day for a general checkup. Part of this checkup required the drawing of her blood. The doctor's phlebotomist, an individual specialized in the drawing of human blood, was not present so instead one of the physician's nurses had to draw my wife's blood. While the nurse had been trained on how to draw blood, it was not something that she did every day, or even every week. As a result, the nurse had a devil of a time drawing my wife's blood. Ultimately, the nurse ended up not being able to draw blood from my wife's arm and had another nurse assist in drawing blood from my wife's hand. The end result was that my wife ended up with her arm and entire hand being severely bruised for several days.

A week or two later, my wife had to revisit that same doctor's office to be run through a specific test where blood had to be drawn four times throughout the procedure. This time, the phlebotomist was in the office and drew the blood for the test. The effects on my wife could not have been more dramatic. Whereas with the nurses drawing the blood just once, my wife ended up with multiple, serious bruises for several days, with the phlebotomist drawing the blood four times, one could barely even see where the blood had been drawn and there was absolutely no bruising.

It struck me that this experience seemed to speak directly to the value of specialists versus generalists. And this is particularly important to IT. The IT industry is a very young field, especially when compared to something like medical services, and specialization has really not come to the forefront in the IT world.

Instead, many in the IT world are generalists. They are able to do lots of things fairly well but nothing particularly well or in-depth. They can do some hardware, they can do some coding and they know how to administer certain systems. They may have a few certain things that they do better than others, but for the most part they are "jacks-of-all-trades".

PROCESS VS. PRODUCT SPECIALIZATION

This jack-of-all-trades mentality is a by-product of how the IT industry sprung-up within business. Businesses, wanting to keep costs low (the IT cost center mentality) hired a single person that could do a little bit of everything. As time wore on, companies hired more and more IT people and could afford a little more specialization, but by and large, the jack-of-all-trades mentality has been maintained in the IT industry. This lack of specialization would seem to be fairly typical of a young profession and is reinforced in the IT industry because many people's first IT jobs are entry level positions in general support roles.

In fact, just how young the IT industry is perhaps best exemplified by its lack of specialization. Of course, there are those out there that are sure to argue with me, pointing to the specialization of some in *Cisco* products or *Microsoft* products or *Novell* products or even so specific a specialization as *Microsoft Exchange*, *Microsoft's* email messaging and collaboration software, but this specialization in specific products is really a poor substitute for true specialization, process specialization.

Consider once again the case of the phlebotomist. The phlebotomist is not a specialist in his or her tools of the trade, the needle and syringe. Instead, the phlebotomist is a specialist of the process of taking blood. If the phlebotomist only knew all about the different types of needles and syringes, he or she would be much less useful. It is great that an individual might know all of the different features of these needles and syringes, but can he or she actually do anything useful with them? By being a specialist in the process of taking blood, the phlebotomist has to learn the tools of the trade. This is because part of being a specialist in the process of taking blood involves knowing what needles and syringes to use in what situations and for what purposes.

I believe that this lack of process specialization is the mark of an extremely young industry although it is also possible that the powerful marketing forces that act upon the IT industry have simply led it astray or that the IT industry is fundamentally flawed due to its focus on products. The reason I believe the former is that the IT industry has in large part simply lacked the need for process specialization until recently. The total knowledge of the IT industry is vast, but is unbelievably small when compared to something like the entire recorded history of the medical industry. And if there is any industry on earth that can give the constantly changing IT industry a run for its money in terms of the pace of innovation, it is most certainly the medical industry. Eventually, the products in the IT industry will become too complex for any single individual to know everything about and the complexity of the systems will make a generalist in those products relatively useless. As this occurs, process specialization will become increasingly important because process will become a useful delineation point in terms of knowledge. Instead of being a specialist in *Microsoft Exchange*, one will need to have a specialist in designing email systems, one in deploying email systems, one in migrating email systems and perhaps one in supporting email systems. The number of fundamental processes surrounding a product is constant and what one does with products, assess, design, deploy, migrate and support are also constant. Therefore, process will become a useful demarcation of knowledge to ensure that the right individuals perform the right processes.

This then speaks to why process specialization has not fully arrived in the IT industry. Most processes performed on a product occur infrequently, unlike with the medical industry where certain processes are performed almost constantly, like drawing blood. The question then becomes, what processes happen with such frequency in the IT industry that a specialist becomes necessary? There is an argument to be made here for basic support and maintenance processes such as performing backups, creating user accounts, etc. and this will be covered a bit later. Outside of support and maintenance, the answer for most businesses is none. There is no reason to keep a specialist in a process such as email migrations or major technology deployments because these types of processes only occur once every five to ten years within any given company. In fact, I would argue that to find true process specialists in the IT industry one has to look almost exclusively at the IT consulting field and even then, process specialization is rare. Even consulting firms do not generally align themselves according to process. They, unfortunately, align themselves according to products and vendors.

But what does this really mean and why is this an important distinction? It is important because having specialized knowledge of a product only extends to the most commonly used features of that product. Someone learning a product like *Microsoft Exchange* may learn the basics of email migration when learning the product, but those skills will not be kept sharp unless they are used with some regularity. Practice makes perfect, if you will. Therefore, relying on generalists for infrequent processes such as email migration can be a painful experience.

Now, one may argue that perhaps the training to become a product specialist would necessarily include the knowledge on how to perform infrequent processes such as deployment or migration. However, even if an individual learns everything there is to know about the process of designing and deploying the system and they deploy the system for a company, how many more times are they going to use that knowledge if they continue to work for that same company. Never. Therefore, the company has essentially spent a lot of time and money to train someone on a process that is now worthless knowledge. What other things could that individual have been doing with his or her time rather than learning knowledge that is now worthless to the company?

So what does this all really mean to the IT world? First, I would argue that the IT world's fascination with product certifications and product specialization is detrimental. To be sure, the IT industry will always need generalists and will always need some type of expertise in products; however, process specialization is a far better indicator of true skills and expertise. Unfortunately, product specialization will likely continue to be important to the IT industry for some time, perhaps forever, because of the IT industry's extreme and misguided emphasis on product. Products are what have built the IT industry. But becoming a specialist in a product only requires that the individual know a small subset of the features and functionality of that product, the ones on the certification tests. Therefore, product certification is a very poor measure of an individual's skills and expertise.

Second, I would argue that the frequency of a particular process is a good criteria to use when deciding whether to perform a process in-house or to hire a consultant. Consultants should be hired when one needs to perform an infrequent process and therefore needs a process expert, not a product expert. The problem with this is that there are too many "consultants" that are nothing more than product specialists and process generalists. Hiring such product specialist consultants adds little value to the organization other than having more warm bodies to execute tasks.

When looking to design, deploy, migrate and support new systems, use consultants that are process specialists, not simply product specialists. There is a difference and knowing the difference will allow a business to hire consultants that bring true value to the business and to a particular IT project. Using process generalists, just like having your blood taken by a nurse instead of a phlebotomist, can leave you bruised and bloodied while using process specialists can make your next major IT project relatively pain free. In addition, by not dedicating internal

IT resources to ramping up on the learning curve posed by infrequent IT processes, a business is not throwing money away by having their valuable resources acquiring knowledge that will be worthless once the project is complete.

OUTSOURCING

So what about IT processes that occur relatively frequently, such as support and maintenance processes? Support and maintenance processes include general system health monitoring and common daily processes such as the creation of network user accounts, changing passwords, performing daily backups, answering end user questions (help desk), performing break/fix hardware maintenance, disposal and many other relatively basic and simple tasks that are repeated at least daily. However, with the possible exception of the largest corporations, most of these "frequent" processes really do not approach the level of frequency and consistency of something like drawing blood in the medical world (our phlebotomist example). Nevertheless, is there an argument to be made that very frequent IT processes should be performed by process specialists?

The fact that these support and maintenance functions are probably the most often outsourced seems to support such an argument. However, I do not support that this is an example of process specialization. Instead, I simply see this as a case of the low-level, repetitive, annoying and menial tasks simply being handed off. In addition, the fact that these functions are often outsourced is more an example of leveraging economies of scale rather than process specialization. So companies do not outsource these functions because they desire process specialists they are simply looking to control costs.

But regardless of why businesses outsource these functions, are the people and/or companies that provide these functions process specialists? Here again, there is an argument to be made to this effect, but I do not believe this is the case. In terms of people, these positions tend to be filled by entry-level, relatively unskilled IT resources. These support tasks require relatively little training and thus do not rise to the level of process specialization. Also, if we take help desk and break/fix work as examples, the respective range of potential questions, issues and hardware requires more of a generalist rather than a specialist. With respect to companies, there is a better case to be made, but I do not believe this is the case. Again, these support and maintenance processes simply lack the requisite skill level to elevate their status to requiring process specialization. In addition, today's IT outsourcing corporations are nowhere near the level of sophistication with regards to process and supporting technology to establish themselves as process specialists in the support and maintenance of IT systems. Therefore, today's large IT outsourcing firms and their employees are not process specialists but are rather simply leveraging economies of scale to provide inexpensive basic support and maintenance services.

PROJECT MANAGEMENT

So, we have explored how infrequent IT processes should be performed by process specialists and not by product specialists or process generalists. In addition, we have seen why many of the more frequent IT processes are often outsourced and not generally handled by internal IT resources. The question naturally arises then as to exactly what internal IT resources should be doing within a business. The rise and prevalence of Project Management within IT answers this question. IT resources tend to perform a lot of projects. But exactly what kinds of projects should they be performing?

8

Opportunity Cost

In order to answer the question posed in the last chapter, "What kinds of projects should internal IT resources be performing?" we must explore one more key business process concept, **Opportunity Cost**.

Opportunity costs are those costs incurred by having resources perform certain processes or tasks in lieu of performing certain other processes or tasks. From an IT consulting perspective, opportunity costs are fairly easy to compute. If a resource that normally bills out at $125/hour is scheduled on a project that only pays $50/hour, the opportunity cost involved is $75/hour, or a yearly opportunity cost of $135,000 ($75/hour * 1800 hours). Now, this opportunity cost must be viewed against certain realities such as whether or not there is $125/hour work for that resource to perform in the same time as the $50/hour work. If not, then $50/hour is better than nothing!

However, opportunity costs are not the sole province of IT consulting or other professional service companies. Every IT shop is a service-oriented organization and while internal resources may have fixed costs, their utilization should be viewed with the same eye toward opportunity costs. Unfortunately, this is not the case in many IT organizations because opportunity cost is not computed within a cost center, which is how IT is viewed by many businesses. Which brings us back to the single, universal and undeniable mission of IT:

The mission of an IT department within a business is to make that business operate more efficiently, effectively and profitably.

So how does this mission have anything to do with opportunity costs? Well, this is where things get tricky and require one to truly embrace the mission of IT within a business versus simply paying it lip service. Truly embracing this mission makes decisions regarding utilization of internal resources elementary but flies in the face of what some might perceive as conventional logic. This can best be shown in an example.

OPPORTUNITY COSTS—AN EXAMPLE

Let's go back to the example of that 200 person, $20,000,000 annual revenue company and speculate that the business wishes to migrate its email system. And we will not get into specific details, suffice to say that this company is migrating one or more email systems to another, single email system and the return on investment analysis has estimated that this migration will save the company some amount of money per year through consolidation of systems and other factors.

Sounds like a no-brainer, right? Saving a business money fits right in line with the IT department's single, universal and undeniable mission, making a business operate more profitably. However, this view actually does not speak to the true mission of IT. What these cost savings represent is a reduction in the cost of the email system, not an introduction of new technology to automate a business process. It is a fine distinction but an important one.

This fine distinction is important because it shows how easy it is to misinterpret the single, universal and undeniable mission of IT. This is proven by the traditional method in which IT departments go about such a migration. To point, if it is estimated that it is going to require 8,000 resource hours to accomplish the migration, the question that naturally arises is the distribution of those hours among available resources. Most companies and IT departments will be interested in accomplishing the migration as inexpensively as possible and thinking they are achieving this goal will dedicate large numbers of internal resources to the task.

In many cases, this is a mistake. The reason this is a mistake is opportunity cost. And the reason this is not caught as a mistake is because internal IT resources are viewed as costs of doing business, a cost center rather than a profit center and thus their opportunity costs are not computed.

To fully understand this, let's continue with the example. Email migrations are not performed very often within companies. Generally, major email migrations occur only once every 5–10 years within any particular business. As such, it makes no sense for an IT department to keep an email migration specialist on staff. Therefore, by dedicating internal IT resources to the email migration, the IT department is likely going to cost the company money, rather than save money. The reason boils down to efficiency. Those 8,000 hours are what the company has estimated it will cost to perform the email migration using internal resources. However, bringing in an email migration specialist to perform this operation is going to be much more efficient because, if a business does its due diligence and hires a competent specialist, that specialist is going to be much more efficient because he or she does not have the learning curve of the internal resources within the IT department who are not email migration specialists.

Let's run some numbers. We will be conservative and estimate that the email migration specialists are only twice as efficient as the non-specialist, internal IT resources. This means that they will accomplish the work in 4,000 hours instead of 8,000 hours. And we will assign a high cost to these email migration specialists, $125/hour. That equates to $500,000 to perform the email migration ($125/hour * 4,000 hours).

Now, we will assign a low cost to internal IT resources of $75,000, fully loaded (salary, benefits, etc.). Using a standard 1,800 hour work year, that equates to a fully loaded hourly cost of $41.67 per productive work hour ($75,000 / 1,800). The product of 8,000 hours at a cost of $41.67 per hour equals $333,360 to perform the email migration.

So far, so good, the overall cost to the company of using internal IT resources is about 2/3rds the cost of using outside resources, even though they are more efficient. However, what is the opportunity cost of those 8,000 hours?

Internal IT resources are specialists in internal IT business systems that support internal business processes. Therefore, what else could these internal IT resources be doing during those 8,000 hours that might save the company money by improving business process efficiencies? This is something that the internal IT resources should be more efficient at than bringing in outside resources. The cost savings of what these internal IT resources could be accomplishing in lieu of learning how to accomplish an email migration, something they are fundamentally ill-suited for, is the opportunity cost to the company. In our example, if that opportunity cost is greater than $500,000 then the company has made a poor decision regarding resource allocation!

But how likely is it that such a cost savings could be realized? That is obviously a matter of conjecture and will vary depending on the situation, but here is one way to look at it. If given 8,000 hours, one would only need to make a 2.5% improvement in overall business efficiency to equal $500,000 ($20,000,000 * 2.5% = $500,000). And, those business process efficiency savings are reoccurring, annual savings unlike the one time savings of performing the email migration internally.

Which sounds like the better deal? I would argue that if given 8,000 hours to analyze and improve a 200 seat business's processes that it is a relatively simple matter to improve the process efficiency of that business by 2.5%. Those 8,000 hours would allow 40 hours with each individual in the company to analyze and improve their micro-processes. And if the results are anything like the phone operator example of saving over $9,000 per year per employee, that equates to $1.8 million saved annually ($9,000 * 200). Over three years, that is $5.4 million in savings. Which sounds better, $5.4 million in savings over 3 years or a one-time savings of a little over $150,000?

And ***that*** is the true power of embracing the single, universal and undeniable mission of IT.

So, am I seriously proposing that a business send its IT people around to sit with their employees and improve their micro-processes? Well, in fact, yes. But we'll get to that in a minute.

9

The Case for Software Development

We have now seen how Specialization and Opportunity Cost can help businesses make decisions about how to allocate internal IT resources. The question that naturally arises is if Specialization and Opportunity Cost argue against IT resources being used for support, maintenance and major IT migration projects, what should those resources be doing with their time? The answer lies in the second canon of IT. You haven't forgotten the second canon of IT have you? In the event that you have, I will save you the trouble of flipping back through to refresh your memory. The second canon of IT is "**IT is about software automating manual tasks**".

THE IMPORTANCE OF SOFTWARE

It is software that makes computers and technology useable by people. People do not think in terms of 0's and 1's like computers. In fact, people and computers are completely foreign to one another in nearly every respect. What bridges the gap and allows people to interact with and harness the power of a computer is software. And the better the software, the better the interface and hence the more power that can be harnessed and leveraged by the end user.

The importance of software in the overall scheme of how technology can help improve business process efficiency cannot be understated. And herein lies the solution to taking a general-purpose tool, the computer, and customizing its operation to provide unique solutions for businesses. Every business is a truly unique organism and consequently every business's processes are also unique. This presents a dilemma for businesses in purchasing and using "shrink-wrapped" software. "Shrink-wrapped" software vendors necessarily make certain simplifications and assumptions in order to make their software applicable to the widest possible number of businesses.

To illustrate this point, let's say that you have an L-shaped cement pad behind your home on which you would like to erect a shed to store lawn equipment and serve as a workshop. One leg of the L-shaped cement pad measures 11'x14' and the other leg measures 8'x11'. Now, if you go out shopping for a pre-fabricated shed, you won't find anything that fits these dimensions. In fact, you will not find any pre-fabricated L-shaped sheds at all. The available pre-fabricated sheds on the market are designed to have as wide an appeal as possible in order to sell the maximum number of units possible. Hence these prefabricated sheds are not going to fully meet all of your custom needs. In addition to the physical structure, this also means that there will be customization required in terms of painting, creation of a workbench, installation of hooks and other odds and ends to get tools off of the floor, etc.

So, knowing that there will be some customization required, you have several options. One option is to buy a pre-fabricated 10'x10' shed and a pre-fabricated 8'x8' shed and live with the sheds as is. This means that you have adapted your needs to what you can find in the market. This may work well for your needs, but at the cost of not utilizing all available space and having two entrances for what you wanted to be a single shed. If you wish to correct this, a second option is to customize the basic pre-fabricated sheds that you purchased by knocking down some walls and extending the sheds as necessary. This customization comes at a cost, but allows you to correct a lot of the annoying inconveniences and better utilize the available space. A third option is to buy the raw materials and custom build the shed to your specifications. By doing this, you are investing your time and energy but are getting exactly what you envisioned, making the most efficient use of the space and potentially saving money if you choose to perform the work yourself.

THE COST OF SUFFICIENT SYSTEMS

So how do sheds have anything to do software development? Well, in this example, quite a bit. Buying shrink-wrapped software is a lot like buying a pre-fabricated shed. The software designers and marketers have made certain simplifications and assumptions intended to create as large an audience as possible for their software. These simplifications and assumptions may or may not meet your needs. In fact, it is almost certain that any business process automation software will not meet all of the specific needs or even translate particularly well to any particular business process.

A good, mild illustration of this is *Quicken*. My business, like thousands of other small businesses, uses *Quicken* to run its books. My business is a consulting services business, meaning we essentially sell people's time. *Quicken*, while a great basic small business accounting package, is really not designed around a services business. Instead, the underlying, simplifying assumptions that the folks at *Quicken* made when designing their software was around the selling of "widgets", manufactured items. While it might first appear that a widget and an hour of time would be roughly equivalent, and in fact, to some extent this equivalency holds, reality is that a services business model really does not translate all that well to a business model designed around selling widgets. Now, one can shoe-horn a services business into *Quicken*, but one has to work around a lot of the simplifying assumptions that the folks at *Quicken* have made regarding what a business does, how a business runs and consequently a business' particular billing and accounting needs. In addition, there are extensive features of *Quicken* that are completely inapplicable. These work-a-rounds translate into business process inefficiencies and the unused features clutter up the user interface making the system more confusing than it needs to be. Therefore, not only are we paying for a bunch of features that are useless, the training costs involved are also increased.

So, just like with a pre-fabricated shed, businesses have similar options when dealing with shrink-wrapped software. They can adapt their business processes to the software, they can customize the software to their particular needs (assuming the software vendors have provided the necessary facilities to allow flexibility, adaptability and customization) or they can custom create the software themselves. It should be noted that two of these three options involve custom software development. In addition, it must be understood that the inconveniences of the software in not being specifically engineered for one's unique business processes translates into reduced business process efficiency, just like using pre-fabricated sheds does not allow you to make the most efficient use of your space. These business process inefficiencies may seem small individually, but when factored into hundreds or thousands of individual business process transactions can result in the loss of thousands or even millions of dollars. Remember that in our running example of a 200 seat, $20,000,000 business that a mere 5% efficiency gain can translate into $1,000,000 of additional profits annually! So if customized software can achieve even a 5% efficiency gain, then is it not worth a significant investment in creating that custom software?

In a competitive business environment, there is little room for business process inefficiencies. These inefficiencies cost real money, which translates into higher prices for the goods and services a business produces. If a business's goods and services are roughly of the same value as their competitors' and business process inefficiencies force the price of their goods and services to be higher than competitors', that business will not be competitive in the market. The inefficiencies of software that is not custom tailored to a business's unique processes is termed **The Cost of Sufficient Systems**. In the business world, it is imperative that software systems that support business processes are as efficient as possible, not just simply sufficient to do the job.

CUSTOM SOFTWARE

Now, the argument that always comes up in this discussion is one of business focus. "We are in the business of making widgets, not writing code." This may seem logical, but such statements are born from a fundamental misunderstanding of one's business and of IT. A business is not in the business of making widgets; a business is in the business of the processes that involve and surround the manufacturing and selling of widgets. As such, making those processes as efficient and effective as possible IS one's business. And, I would argue that a business cannot make its business processes as efficient and effective as possible without custom software development, whether that is the customization of shrink-wrapped software or the building of that software from scratch. Hence, custom software development is a crucial, core competency of all businesses. This is not because every business is a software development business, but because every business is in the business of making its business processes as efficient and effective as possible. In fact, if done properly, the customized business process software actually becomes the business processes. *Custom software that improves, automates and makes a business process efficient and effective becomes the embodiment and physical manifestation of that business process.*

Another argument in favor of custom software deals with leveraging IT to beat one's competition. If every business uses the exact same software to run their business processes, then there can be no competitive advantage to a business's IT systems. If everyone runs the same software, then everyone is paying the same price for that software and everyone must deal with the same limitations and headaches of that software. There is no competitive advantage. For some things, like word processing software, this is fine, but not for business process software that helps determine how effective, efficient and profitable a business becomes. A competitive advantage can be obtained by running custom software that can be optimized to make it more efficient and effective than using the same shrink-wrapped code that every other business is using.

Finally, no discussion regarding custom software development would be complete without a discussion regarding "proprietary systems". Proprietary systems are those systems created by a software vendor that in some way tie a business to that particular software vendor. This is most often the result of the use of proprietary data systems, a proprietary "framework" in which one develops and customizes the software or a "closed system", one that is designed around generic business processes common to a particular industry such as medical or manufacturing.

Now, to be clear, by proprietary systems, I am generally referring to database systems. Nearly all business process systems are database systems. And I only use the qualifying "nearly" because I like to avoid absolutes. Business processes necessarily involve the management of some kind of information. The work of managing the data of business processes falls to our old friend, the database. While nearly all databases are inherently tied to some vendor, the more proprietary the database, the fewer options one has for querying, storing and retrieving information from that database. Systems like *Microsoft Access* or *Lotus Notes* are less proprietary than some other systems because they include the ability to access the data through non-proprietary, standards-based mechanisms, such as ODBC (Open Database Connectivity) or SQL (Structured Query Language) queries. It is imperative that the database systems used within a business have standards-based mechanisms by which to access the data because without such access, it becomes nearly impossible to migrate data from the database in a cost-effective way.

Frameworks are probably the best option for businesses considering shrink-wrapped software for business process software development. Frameworks typically do not "do" anything but instead provide a, well, "framework" for development. In other words, the framework allows businesses to use it to more easily build their business process applications by combining pre-defined objects and code. However, at the heart of all frameworks are particular assumptions and limitations with regards to the business process applications built within the framework. As long as the business process applications built within the framework adhere to these underlying assumptions all is well with the world. Step outside of these underlying assumptions and the framework becomes a hindrance instead of a help. In fact, in many cases using a framework for an application that violates an underlying assumption or hits a particular limitation can make it almost impossible to finish the application. *Lotus Notes* was, and to some extent still is, notorious for hitting this brick wall of development. One could quickly develop 80% of a business process application, but the last 20% would often leave developers banging their heads against and through a wall.

Extremely proprietary systems, closed systems, such as those used heavily in the medical field, many times lock a corporation into the software's particular way of doing things and can even force corporations into a technological dead-end by not allowing the easy migration of data within those systems to new, improved systems that more accurately reflect the business processes of a company. In this way, proprietary systems can cost businesses thousands or even millions of dollars, especially if old systems must be kept around long after the business processes those systems supported have been improved and changed. Closed systems are often the worst possible choice for shrink-wrapped software and should generally be avoided. The word plague comes to mind. A business that buys a proprietary, closed system, is essentially locking itself into a particular vendor or even a particular process until the end of time. This means that a business is adopting someone else's process, the software vendor's instead of the one that is the most efficient, effective and profitable for the business.

To summarize, businesses need to ensure that the software systems that embody their business processes can be easily migrated and facilitate the ability to improve and customize the system as their business processes improve. The most efficient and effective way to accomplish this is to build or customize business process software that sits on top of open data standards. Frameworks are an acceptable choice as long as one is confident that the framework is flexible enough to meet the needs of the business and the business processes that will be automated match the underlying assumptions and structure of the framework. Closed, proprietary systems should generally be avoided.

10

Beyond Code

We now know that internal IT resources should be spending their time automating manual business processes through the effective use of custom software development instead of performing tasks for which they are not specialized and which have a significant opportunity cost. The picture of how to actually go about improving a business's processes is nearly complete. However, there is one final piece of the puzzle that is still missing. This missing piece is directly addressed by the third canon of IT; **IT must be useable**. In order to fill in the remaining piece of the puzzle, IT must go beyond its tools of computers and digital systems, beyond mere software coding and, in fact, go beyond IT itself. IT must engage in and with the actual business processes and the people performing those processes.

There is a scenario that I have seen repeated over and over again with dozens of businesses. Because of the fundamental misunderstanding of IT as a cost center, businesses become preoccupied with minimizing IT operational costs. This, without fail, leads to a global IT standardization project in which all servers and desktops within the business are standardized to a single operating system, standard software, etc. These kinds of projects are extremely expensive; with many corporations choosing to standardize hardware, operating systems and application software all in one fell swoop. Now, these projects always start out with a healthy training budget that invariably is significantly reduced or even eliminated. This breaks IT canon #3; IT must be useable.

Let's take another look at that $20,000,000 business that employs 200 individuals. Let's say that this business undertakes an IT standardization project similar to what I have described above. What if deploying that new technology without training reduces the ability of the employees to accomplish their business processes by just 1%? Now, to be clear, I will even grant that the overall effect of deploying the new system has a net positive effect on overall efficiency since the standardized systems should be much more reliable and supportable. The arguments for standardization are that it leads to better systems, better support and less down time, allowing users to get more work accomplished with fewer hassles. But regardless of any efficiencies and cost savings gained by deploying these new systems, the lack of training almost certainly ensures that the full potential of the new systems to improve business process efficiency is not fully realized. If this lack of training causes only a 1% reduction in the net effectiveness of the new systems, that translates to a cost of $200,000. $200,000 would pay for $1,000 worth of training per each employee. That is quite a bit of training. That means that one could have a trainer billing at a rate of $100/hour sit with each employee for 10 hours. (10 hours * 100/hour * 200) Ten hours of individual, one-on-one training is probably more training on technology than those employees have received during their entire tenure with that company. Think of the business process efficiencies that could be gained from such training!

TECHNOLOGY LIASONS

But, this raises a larger issue in terms of training and end users. Many end users and divisions within corporations know relatively little about technology. This is not because they are dumb or any other stereotypical IT mentality, it is because no one has ever bothered to show or teach them anything. They are not the technology experts; they simply do not know what they do not know. They have no basis to understand just exactly what can be accomplished through the full utilization of technology. I can significantly improve the business process efficiency of end users by simply showing them how to use hot keys, a few simple tricks in *Microsoft Word* and *Excel* or features of their proprietary systems that they never even knew existed! These simple little tricks, believe it or not, can significantly improve business process efficiency. They can take tasks that previously took hours and compress them down to mere minutes.

And this speaks to the third canon of IT and its implications for IT departments. One of the chief responsibilities of every IT department in every company must be to inform and educate end users and teach them how to use the technology they are given. It is not sufficient to excuse it away with "They'll figure it out." or "They know what they are supposed to be doing better than I do." or any other excuse. IT is the center of technological expertise and it is IT's responsibility to see how the end users are utilizing the technology and then show them how to use it more effectively and efficiently. Without IT's guidance, how can departments and individuals be expected to pick the right/best technology for a business that not only fulfills the business needs but also the long term, strategic technological and support needs as well?

What I am getting at is that one of the primary job responsibilities for IT personnel should be to serve as technology liaisons to end-users. IT personnel should sit with each and every employee within a business and watch how the employees use technology as well as how they accomplish their manual tasks or micro-processes. Then, those IT personnel should show the end users how to use technology more efficiently and effectively and take notes about the manual processes those end users perform in order to see how the processes might be automated.

Unfortunately, the trend in the IT industry is towards more and more consolidation, a return to the mainframe "glass house", only this time with PC's. This trend toward more and more consolidated systems is leading to the centralization of IT services and personnel in order to control costs. However, this takes IT resources away from the people that IT needs to be serving. If the tools experts are not at a location and intimately familiar with the daily business processes of the corporation, how can they lend their tools expertise to solving business problems and issues? They cannot.

AN EXAMPLE

To demonstrate, I worked for an electric power company in Ohio during a few summers while I was attending college for my mechanical engineering undergraduate degree. I had been involved in computers since the age of 13 on my trusty *Tandy 1000 EX*, had self-taught myself most of my programming skills and had played a key role in, literally, building my college's campus-wide network from the ground up including splicing fiber, digging trenches for network cables and pulling cables through crawlspaces and drop ceilings. The work with the electric company was mostly sheer boredom. I spent most of the first summer tracing maps, checking electric poles and other various odd jobs. I basically got to know lots of pieces of lots of different parts of the business. The office that I worked for was a pretty small office in Marion, OH and I considered it horribly technologically deficient. There were only two computers in the entire office and one simply sat idle all day. Everything was paper-based and a manual process. I was bored stiff and in abject shock from the lack of technology. But one piece of the business caught my eye, originally because it was an interesting Statics problem. Statics is the engineering discipline of studying mechanical systems that do not move, i.e. they are static.

The problem involved electric poles at the end of a row or at a corner. These poles needed to have a guy wire run from the pole to a metal anchor that screwed into the ground in order to keep the pole from falling over due to the weight of the electric wires supported by the pole. No one typically ever pays attention or really even notices these structures, but take a look sometime, they are everywhere, their variations nearly endless and they are really pretty interesting. OK, maybe not, but I like them. Now, I will not bore you with the gory details, but suffice it to say that the problem of how far away from the pole to place the anchor is a statically indeterminate problem. That is a fancy way of saying that the problem has more unknowns than equations available to solve it. And in plain English that means that you have to guess where to place the anchor, literally. You make an educated guess, solve the set of equations and if the anchor is too close to the pole, one of the results of the equations will be too high a value, such as too high a stress on the guy or too high a stress vertically on the pole. So, if one of the numbers is too high, you then have to guess a new number and solve the equations all over again. This process could easily take 30–45 minutes and really tricky problems involving multiple guys, multiple anchors, multiple wires and even multiple poles could take much, much longer.

I decided that this was ridiculous and convinced one of my managers to let me take a shot at automating the process using a computer. I mean, gee, a process involving a series of calculations that must be repeated over and over until certain conditions are met? The problem was begging for a computer! So I wrote a program in *Microsoft QuickBASIC* where they could enter the parameters of the pole structure and it would iterate through and automatically solve the problem. Furthermore, the program allowed the end user to "play" with the result by changing any parameter and letting the system immediately recalculate the result. Hmm, beginning to sound an awful lot like a spreadsheet…The program allowed even very complex guying problems involving multiple guys, multiple anchors, multiple wires and even multiple poles to be solved, literally, as fast as one could enter the parameters into the computer.

The point of this example is that if I had not been sitting with and learning about the manual tasks of the business, I would never have observed this process and been able to offer a solution. Unless a business's IT personnel are out among the people performing the daily business operations, they cannot help educate those people and they certainly cannot comprehend the manual tasks that those people are performing. If they are not educating, then they are not making IT useable and if they are not observing, then they will never be able to automate manual tasks through software. By not using IT personnel as technology liaisons,

IT automatically fails at two of the three canons of IT, making IT useable and using software to automate manual tasks. And if IT is not useable and is not automating manual tasks, then IT fails at the third IT canon, making economic sense.

11

The Process of Change

The IT world as it exists today is one founded on the worship of the Tool, the next new and exciting hardware platform or the latest shrink-wrapped software. It is a world of monolithic, tyrannical standards bodies that centralize themselves into glass houses and tune out the rest of the world. It is a world where computers are considered a cost of doing business and IT departments are simply cost centers, a drain on the profitability of a business.

What IT should be is a dynamic and engaging organization that reaches out to the individual business units that own the business processes of a corporation. IT should be showing individuals, business units and businesses the power of technology to solve and eliminate their most pressing business problems. IT should be creating systems custom tailored to a corporation's unique business processes in order to maximize business process efficiency, reduce costs and increase profitability.

The question becomes, how does a business and IT department move from where it is today to what it should be?

The solution to transforming IT from a cost center to a profit center is, and this should come as no big surprise, first and foremost a process. This process will take different companies different lengths of time to implement and is truly a never-ending process of change. But, only by committing to the process of change and living it day to day will a business ever truly have a hope of transforming IT from a cost center to a profit center.

The process is not easy and will not happen overnight. It is likely that some companies will try, fail and revert back to the same old ways of doing IT. Other companies will pay it lip service and do nothing to truly effect change. Still others will perhaps find a comfortable "rest area" along the path and stay there indefinitely. But, for those companies and IT departments that truly believe in the power of IT as a profit center and truly believe in and want to achieve process profitability, the rest of this book is written specifically for you.

THE IT COST CENTER

To start, let us create a visual map of a business where IT is simply a cost center. If we take our concentric circles, People, Process, Tool view of a business and map in the common departments within a business, we get something that looks like the following diagram:

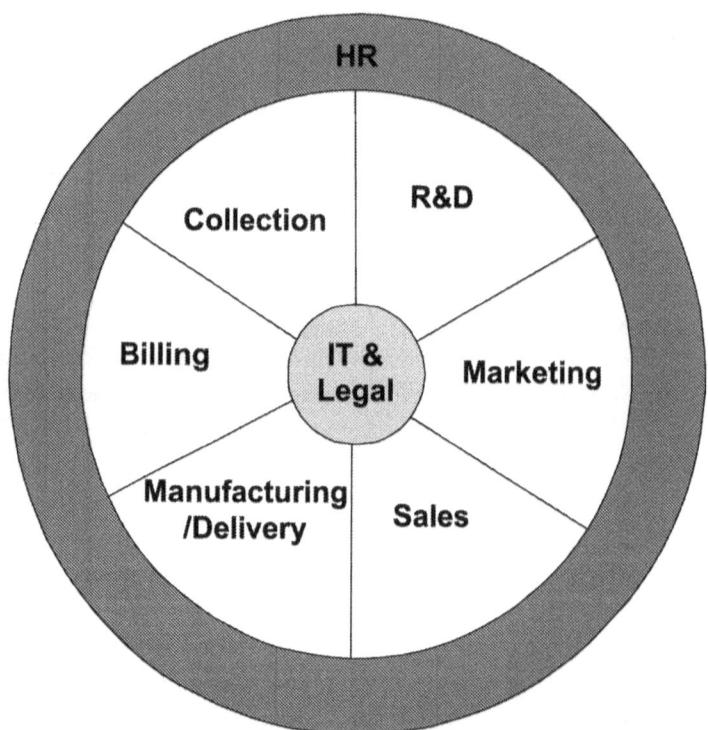

Figure 12: The IT Cost Center

As one can see, the various, common individual departments within a company by and large fall into the Process ring, meaning that the various divisions, departments and organizational units within a business are roughly aligned along individual business processes, Marketing, Sales, Manufacturing, etc. The odd departments out are HR, IT and Legal. HR falls into the People ring since its purpose is to manage all of the people aspects of a business, hiring, benefits, etc. IT and Legal fall into the Tool ring. This may seem odd considering that both IT and Legal are service-based professions, but to a business, they are simply tools that can be brought to bear to solve particular business problems. This is the world of the IT cost center, where IT is isolated as a cost of doing business.

THE IT PROFIT CENTER

Now, let's look at how the picture changes as one creates the IT Profit Center. To be sure, IT will still have a more or less fixed cost component that is left in the center of the diagram. This represents the hardware, licensing and maintenance costs of IT. However, the IT Profit Center extends out beyond this classic world of IT and becomes an integral part of the individual business units.

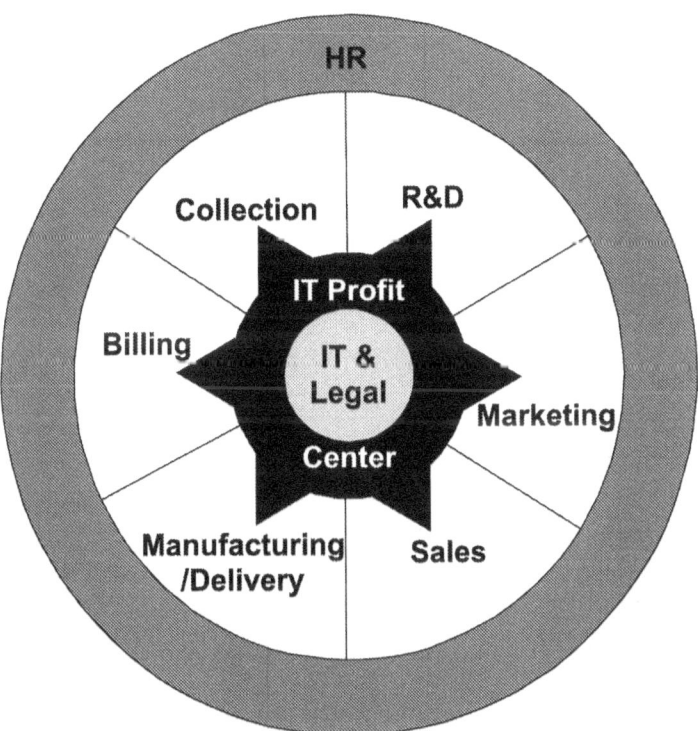

Figure 13: The IT Profit Center

FROM COST CENTER TO PROFIT CENTER—TRANSFORMING IT

Now that we have a good visual model for the IT Profit Center, we are still left with the problem of how to transform one's current IT Cost Center into an IT Profit Center. To get from cost center to profit center, we must first recognize what not to do. Chief among those things not to do is to try to do everything at once. This transformation will not occur in a day or six months or a year. Change is difficult. Years of doing IT badly have created a virtual prison for many corporations that fundamentally works against change. The primary reason is that asset allocation decisions made under the previous premise of IT is a cost center are no longer valid, but a business is stuck with gradually phasing out those asset allocation decisions. Another reason is because of the personnel within IT. Under previous assumptions about IT, certain personnel decisions were made that reflected the perceptions and attitudes of IT held at that time. While perceptions and attitudes may have changed, the personnel hired previously have not. Therefore, a reeducation process is required among IT personnel and some personnel will simply lack the skills required to cut it in the brave new IT profit center world. So, first and foremost, prepare for the long haul and think evolutionary change, not revolutionary change.

This evolution starts with management buy-in. This includes buy-in from IT management and, in particular, "C" level management, as in CEO, CFO, etc. With all appropriate apologies for shameless self-promotion, ensure that everyone involved in the IT decision-making process from the CEO on down reads this book and understands the three canons of IT, as well as the single, universal and undeniable mission of IT. This is of crucial importance, because true, lasting change can only come from the top of a business. Every manager in the organization must understand, believe in, and become an advocate of the IT Profit Center.

Once a business has management buy-in, the next step is to take the message to the IT personnel. Make an honest and critical assessment of IT personnel skills. The skills of primary importance in an IT profit center are software development and scripting skills as well as communication skills. This does not mean that there is no place for IT personnel that lack these skills but those that lack skills in software development and communication are not going to aid in the transformation of IT from a cost center to a profit center.

Do not be discouraged if IT personnel lack good, interpersonal communication skills. Lack of interpersonal communication skills is a common failing of those within IT. Let's face it, IT personnel have chosen to work with computers, not people and thus many have never developed effective interpersonal communication skills. Fear not, effective communication skills can be taught. For example, in my business, we have taken individuals that literally simply wanted to be locked in a dark room and code and taught them effective communication skills and how to interact with clients. And, along with the headaches, they have found great rewards and now appreciate the value, both personal and professional, of interacting with clients. Thus, begin a program to aid IT personnel with their communication skills. Effective interpersonal communication skills are an absolute requirement if one expects these resources to begin interacting with other individuals within one's business.

Also, do not be overly concerned about a lack of good software development skills. If solid software development skills are lacking, then focus on simple programming skills such as batch programming or scripting. There are huge numbers of business process problems that can be automated with very simple scripting in *Visual Basic, Perl* or even in *DOS* batch files and these skills are easy to pick up. If tackling a critical, complex business process application, then look to outside developers with skills in more complex and powerful programming languages as well as the skills to create object oriented, supportable code.

The most effective method of promoting change within IT is to actually make internal IT personnel actually live process improvement. By living and breathing process efficiency, IT personnel will truly understand at an intuitive level what the business is trying to accomplish and why. It is only through understanding the power of process in their daily lives that they will become advocates for process and change their attitudes towards the business units/departments. And how does one make IT personnel live, breath and eat process? Simple, make them focus on their own daily processes and begin codifying and automating those processes. As IT personnel document the processes that they perform each day, work with them to improve, simplify, document and automate those processes.

As more and more of the daily IT support and maintenance processes are documented, simplified and automated, the natural effect will be to free up IT resources that would normally be engaged in the manual completion of those tasks. As IT processes become simpler and more automated, companies should seriously consider outsourcing these processes or otherwise finding relatively low skilled, low paid resources to complete these now mundane chores.

Once IT resources are freed up, they have now seen firsthand the power of process in their own world of IT, they are no longer tied down performing the same drudgery day after day, and they should now have some more effective communication skills that will give them the confidence they need to interact with individuals within other segments of the business. This then provides an opportunity to send them out into the individual business units/departments to observe and document the manual business processes that are occurring within specific business units. But before sending these resources out into the field, make absolutely certain that IT personnel are prepared with the proper attitude and communication skills. Part of this should be education and training on **The Consultative Approach** as outlined in **Appendix A**. The Consultative Approach is a key component in preparing IT resources to productively interact with individuals within business units or departments.

Once these IT resources have seen the power of process within their own work lives and are prepared with the proper attitude and communication skills, these IT resources can now be released into the individual business units to look for manual processes that are similar to the types of processes that they have already documented and automated. They have already been through the process and thus can serve as guides and advocates of the process for the individuals within the business units whose lives and work they are helping to simplify and improve.

At this point, one must be careful not to let the floodgates open just yet. And the flood will come. Once IT resources specifically looking for process improvements are released into the individual business units, the number and type of business process improvement ideas generated by these resources and by the individual business units themselves will become a veritable torrent. The next step is to pilot business process improvement within the company. So how does a company go about finding, analyzing and improving business processes? The quick answer to this question, to paraphrase the environmentalists, is to "Think macro-ly and act micro-ly."

While it may make a good theoretical argument that improving everyone's business process efficiency at a micro-level will improve the business process efficiency of a company, the theory must be tempered by reality. Reality is that businesses are going to have certain components of their business that operate more efficiently than others and are more crucial to the success of their business than others. In addition, reality dictates that companies are not going to have the cash flow necessary to improve all of their business at once. To combat the realities of business, one must establish priorities regarding which processes to attack first. This involves analyzing one's business from a macro level and finding the area of the business that has the most egregious business process inefficiencies, or has the processes where improvement will translate into the most money saved or has the processes that serve as bottlenecks to the rest of a business.

Bottlenecks at the macro level are particularly important because they point to an area of a business, which, if improved, will translate into increased output and efficiency for the entire business. A bottleneck, by definition, is an area that is constraining or holding a business back because the other components of the business can handle an increased load. Therefore, if one wants to impact the entire business, all one has to do is find and eliminate that bottleneck. Unfortunately, this is easier said than done. Regardless, the output of a macro-level analysis and analysis of feedback from IT personnel within individual departments will be the identification of a particular business segment that is of particular interest to a business with regards to improving its business process efficiencies.

The next step is to take that business segment and similarly analyze its mezzo-level business processes, those business processes particular to that individual business segment. This is a good time to begin introducing the concept of corporate memory and its associated mechanisms of senses, cycles, and feedback, in order to capture and analyze those business processes. One of the first assignments or projects assigned to IT resources in the field should be a way of capturing the required metrics regarding the business processes of interest.

This analysis will likely lead to a discussion regarding how custom software can improve the mezzo-level business processes. This is a good discussion and path to pursue, but do not let it distract from delving into the micro-processes of individuals. This step is crucial because this provides the most "bang for the buck". It is almost a certainty that simply taking a look at the micro-level tasks of individuals and showing those individuals how to use their existing technology more efficiently and effectively can improve the business processes of a particular business segment. One will be amazed at the efficiency gains that can be made simply by showing individuals simple concepts such as "hot keys" and other simple tricks that will improve efficiency. Having IT personnel integrated within each individual business unit is absolutely necessary in achieving this result. In addition, acting micro-ly allows small pieces of the overall problem to be singled out and solved without being dragged into a huge, complex and high-profile project. Biting off more than one can chew is a common reason for IT project failure and should be avoided.

As these micro-level, mezzo and finally macro business process improvements are put into effect, resources of time and people will naturally free up. One must take a hard look at these resources to see how they can be leveraged within a business segment or applied to other aspects of a business. This creates a ripple-effect that will be felt throughout an individual business segment and a business as a whole.

Once the effects of this process are completed for an individual business segment and the resource allocation ripple achieves steady state, the process starts all over again. This may occur while still involved in a custom development project to further improve the business processes of the first business segment so be sure not to over extend IT resources. By delving into the micro-processes of a business, IT personnel will uncover an endless number of improvements that can be made through the creation of custom software that automates and improves the efficiency of a business's unique business processes. The list will quickly become overwhelming, so pick those that will have the greatest impact on the business and dedicate IT resources to creating and putting those systems in place while still leaving enough IT resources free to continue with the day-to-day assistance and delivery of expertise directly to individuals within the individual business units.

As the list of business process improvements grows and a business analyzes each of these opportunities to increase the profitability of the business, IT departments will be forced to make IT resource allocations. Make those resource allocations based on the three canons of IT and the single, universal and undeniable mission of IT. Slowly, a business and its IT department will become focused on the right projects and no longer engage in the wrong projects.

Engaging in this continual process of business process improvement is the only way to truly change an IT organization from a cost center to a profit center because it forces both IT and a business to truly live by the tenets and concepts proposed here versus simply paying them lip service.

The Three Canons of IT:

1.   IT must make economic sense

2.   IT is about software automating manual tasks

3.   IT must be useable

The Single, Universal and Undeniable Mission of IT:
The mission of an IT department within a business is to make that business operate more efficiently, effectively and PROFITABLY.

This is it, no big finale or "silver bullet" revelation. I have presented the roadmap that will move a business and IT department from the defunct and broken world of the IT Cost Center focused on Tools and take those dedicated to the process of change to the world of the IT Profit Center focused on business process solutions. I will leave the reader with this simple statement. *If you believe in the concepts expressed in this book and dedicate yourself to the cause, you can build the IT Profit Center and it will bring your business greater efficiency, effectiveness and PROFITABILITY.*

Appendix A:
The Consultative Approach

There really is no secret to the consultative approach. In fact, the consultative approach itself is fairly obvious and self-explanatory. However, actually following the consultative approach is not quite so easy because of one extremely important aspect of human nature, opinion. Opinions, while important to have, must be watched extremely closely by anyone following the consultative approach because strong opinions may slant or bias the results from one's execution of the consultative approach. This is not to say that opinions are necessarily a bad thing. However, forming strong opinions about the task at hand is best kept until the end of the consultative approach. The best opinions are supported by unbiased evidence and facts collected during the consultative approach and are never forced upon the client.

This appendix lays out the consultative approach in form and function, first describing the components of the consultative approach and then describing the steps to complete an exercise in the consultative approach. This appendix is intended as an introduction to the consultative approach as well as a quick reference for those executing the consultative approach.

THE COMPONENTS

There are four basic components of the consultative approach:

1. The Need
2. The Client
3. The Consultant
4. The Solution

THE NEED

The need is some problem that requires a solution. This can be any problem or issue under the sun. Without a need, there is no reason for the consultative approach. Therefore, the need is the impetus for engaging in the consultative approach.

THE CLIENT

The client is quite simply the party that has the need. Usually, the client has some vested interest in seeing his or her need resolved. In addition, the client generally has intimate knowledge regarding his or her need and potentially some rough ideas on how to solve or meet that need.

THE CONSULTANT

First of all, one does not need to be a "consultant" to fulfill the consultant's role. The consultant is simply the individual executing the consultative approach. The consultant is often an expert problem solver in a particular area, although the consultative approach does not require that the consultant be an expert in the particular need. In fact, the consultant's role is to execute the consultative approach by extracting the client's intimate knowledge of the need and performing the necessary research to become an expert in the various solutions to the need.

THE SOLUTION

The solution is the end goal of the consultative approach. There are two extremely important aspects to the solution. First, every time a consultative approach is engaged in, there must be a solution; otherwise the consultative approach has not been completed. That does not mean that the need is always resolved. Therefore, the solution may be that there is currently no way to resolve the need. Second, the client must ultimately agree with the solution.

THE CONSULTATIVE PROCESS

There are four basic steps to the consultative approach:

1. Listen
2. Learn
3. Look
4. List

STEP ONE: LISTEN

Step One is the most important of all of the steps in the consultative approach. Unless the consultant is willing to listen to the client without bias, the consultative approach cannot proceed. Consultants that do not succeed at the consultative approach invariably skip step one. Listen to the client describe his or her need. Write down the need. Listen and document why the client has this need and what the client has done in the past to help remedy this need.

STEP TWO: LEARN

Learning is where the consultant extracts the client's intimate knowledge of the problem. The consultant must not assume anything with regard to the need. Only the client has the full knowledge of need and in general, clients are not skilled at articulating their needs. Therefore, the consultant must carefully structure inquiries in order to extract all possible knowledge from the client. In addition, the consultant must pay close attention to details.

The two main items of knowledge that the consultant must extract are the needs and the constraints.

The Needs

The needs are the reason for engaging in the consultative approach. The client, because of his or her intimate involvement with the needs, generally has a skewed view of the needs. This is to say that the client generally has a tendency to gloss over the real need and focus on the effects of the need. In addition, certain needs are more important than others to the client but the client may not be able to express this effectively. The consultant must carefully rank the needs and identify the most critical needs.

The Constraints

Constraints are the items that help define and weed-out solutions. Again, clients may or may not think in terms of constraints and so the consultant must pay close attention to any and all constraints. Constraints can be anything and everything, from the current operating system of a computer to the software a client "feels comfortable" with. A solution that meets the needs but does not fall within the constraints is no solution at all. As with needs, the consultant must pay close attention to the ranking or importance of constraints. A good solution may be able to bend a few low ranking constraints.

STEP THREE: LOOK

Once everything has been learned about the needs and constraints, the consultant must now research and analyze any and all possible solutions. Here again, the consultant must be wary to set aside opinion and bias. All possible solutions should be explored regardless of the consultant's own opinions on their ultimate feasibility. Remember, a bad solution will be easily recognizable by its weaknesses with regards to needs and constraints while a good solution will be just as evident by its strengths. However, the consultant must never simply exclude a solution from analysis due to his or her own opinions. This leads to an incomplete analysis and ultimately a poor presentation of solutions.

STEP FOUR: LIST

Once all research is complete, each potential solution should be listed. Included in the list should be an overview of each solution as well as its strengths and weaknesses. Don't reinvent the wheel. Look for existing code and solutions that have solved similar problems. Only in the absence of, or after determining the inadequacy of, existing solutions should custom solutions be explored. This list of solutions should be presented to the client and the client should be allowed to make the final decision as to the correct solution. The consultant can have his or her opinions, should serve as expert technology advisor and should vehemently defend against the client doing anything self destructive, but ultimately it is the client's decision.

SUMMARY

The consultative approach, while easy to understand and fairly self-explanatory, is often difficult to execute correctly because opinions and bias get in the way of listening to the client and performing a fair and exhaustive review of potential solutions.

Individuals engaging in the consultative approach should constantly remind themselves to listen to the client free of personal opinion and bias. Expert, rational argumentation for or against a particular solution is fine, but must be done only after listening, learning and looking. And ultimately, the final decision on the right solution is the client's. Once the consultative approach has arrived at a solution, the final step is to actually build and implement the solution.

0-595-28970-3

www.ingramcontent.com/pod-product-compliance
Lightning Source LLC
Chambersburg PA
CBHW021003180526
45163CB00005B/1878